Naval Customs and Traditions
Second Edition

Gerard Wells

WITH ILLUSTRATIONS

The way of Great Britain is on the sea, for we are a small island in the midst of the sea. The stock of our people came dashing across the sea: its defence and its highroads have been the sea; its flag is a flag of the sea. Our Navy is no superfluity to us. It is us.
Mr. Ramsay MacDonald's speech of January 21st, 1930

Solis Press

Impossible!!
A hateful word, usually supplanted among good seamen by "We'll try."
The Sailor's Word Book (Smyth).

Photo and image acknowledgements: page 11 Collectorofinsignia/Wikipedia, http://creativecommons.org/licenses/by-sa/3.0/; pages 12, 22 Wikipedia; page 25 Wikimedia Commons; pages 30, 34 Wikipedia; page 36 Wikimedia Commons; page 49 Robert Gray; page 52 *top* © Bill Bertram 2006, http://creativecommons.org/licenses/by/2.5/, *bottom* Dave Jenkins from www.defenceimages.mod.uk/ Reproduced under the terms of the Open Government License www.nationalarchives.gov.uk/doc/open-government-licence/; pages 55, 57, 64 Wikipedia; pages 65, 68, 71 Wikimedia Commons; pages 77, 82 *top* Wikipedia; pages 82 *bottom*, 84 Wikimedia Commons; page 85 Wikipedia; page 87 United States Navy ID 051129-N-0685C-007; page 89 Wikipedia; page 95 Library of Congress Prints and Photographs Division Washington, D.C. 20540 USA; page 100 Dr Neil Clifton, http://creativecommons.org/licenses/by-sa/2.0/deed.en; page 101 National Maritime Museum via Flickr Commons; page 106 Project Gutenberg; page 109 Tam McDonald from www.defenceimages.mod.uk Reproduced under the terms of the Open Government License www.nationalarchives.gov.uk/doc/open-government-licence/; page 112 Wikimedia Commons. Public domain images reproduced under this licence: http://creativecommons.org/publicdomain/mark/1.0/

Every effort has been made to trace all copyright holders. If any have been inadvertently overlooked the publisher will be pleased to make any necessary amendments at the first opportunity.

First published in 1930. This second edition with additional marginal images published by Solis Press, 2014.

Typographical arrangement copyright © Solis Press 2014

All rights reserved. No part of this publication may be reproduced, stored in a retrieval system, or transmitted, in any form or by any means, electronic, mechanical, photocopying, recording or otherwise, except as permitted by the UK Copyright, Designs and Patents Act 1988, without the prior permission of the publisher.

This book is sold subject to the condition that it shall not, by way or trade or otherwise, be lent, resold, hired out or otherwise circulated without the publisher's prior consent in any form of binding or cover other than in which it is published and without a similar condition including this condition being imposed on the subsequent purchaser.

ISBN: 978-1-910146-03-3

Published by Solis Press, PO Box 482, Tunbridge Wells TN2 9QT, Kent, England

Web: www.solispress.com | *Twitter*: @SolisPress

Contents

Introduction 4

Biographical Note 4

List of Illustrations 5

Naval Customs and Traditions 6

Introduction

Although lectures have been given, from time to time, on the origins of the customs and traditions of the Royal Navy, little attempt has been made to present them in book form, and I hope that the publication of this book will lead to further research and collection.

I wish to express my warmest thanks for their advice and help, to Professor Geoffrey Callender of the Royal Naval College, Greenwich, and to Mr. D. B. Smith of the Admiralty Library; also to Mr. P. W. Morehen of the Lantern Lecture Department, Royal Naval College, Greenwich, for his most valuable assistance; also to Mrs. MacIlwaine for permission to reproduce various naval expressions from a collection made by the late Captain George S. MacIlwaine, Royal Navy. I am greatly indebted to the Trustees of the Macpherson Collection for their permission to reproduce engravings from the collection.

To the Society of Nautical Research and to the Council of the Royal United Service Institution I am especially grateful, for permission to quote largely from *The Mariner's Mirror* and United Service Institution Journals respectively.

Also to Commander C. N. Robinson for permission to use his book *The British Fleet*.

Gerard Wells

Biographical Note

GERARD AYLMER WELLS
6 October 1879 – 8 August 1943

Naval Cadet	15 January 1893
Midshipman	15 September 1895
Sub-Lieutenant	15 March 1899
Lieutenant	30 June 1901
Commander	30 June 1913
Captain	30 June 1918
Rear-Admiral	1 October 1929
Retired	11 October 1930
Vice-Admiral (promoted in retirement)	16 January 1935
Director General of Ports and Lighthouses Administration, Egypt	1932–43
Awarded Knight Commander of the Most Excellent Order of the British Empire (KBE)	1937

List of Illustrations

A Mid – On Half Pay, 1827	cover
A First Rate Man of War, taken from the Dock Yard, Plymouth, 1809	9
Weighing Anchor	12
Portsmouth Point, 1814	19
A Chip of the Old Block	29
A Greenwich Pensioner, 1828	51
The Interior of a Midshipman's Berth, 1821	54
A Midshipman, 1823	67
A Midshipman, 1828	69
The Sailor's Progress	83
Common Sailor, 1828	104
Costume of the Royal Navy, 1847, Captain, Flag Officer, and Commander (undress)	108

Admiral

Title derived from the Arabic '*Amir-al-Bahr,*' translated 'Admiral of the Seas,' *Bahr* being, in the course of time, dropped. The Amir Admirals were styled '*Sarracenorum Admirati,*' which may explain how the 'd' was introduced into the Latinised form of *Amiral*.

The title appears in England in 1297, when William de Leyburn, hitherto styled 'Captain of the King's Mariners,' was made 'Admiral of the Sea of the King of England' by Edward I. The title was later given to two Admirals, one for the northern parts – i.e. ships belonging to ports between the mouth of the Thames and Berwick-on-Tweed – the other for the western ports, which included all the rest of England, and more especially the Cinque Ports.

The first extant Royal Commission to a British Naval Officer was in 1303, when Gervase Alard was appointed Captain and Admiral.

The title of 'Captain' probably conferred executive command; that of 'Admiral' conferred legal powers, devolved by the Lord High Admiral.

The last Captain and Admiral appointed was Sir Reginald Cobham in 1344.

After this date the title of Admiral only was given usually as a temporary rank whilst in command of the fleet or fleets.

In the sixteenth and seventeenth centuries, when the titles Captain and Admiral were used, Captain referred to the chief officer in command, and Admiral to his flag-ship, Vice-Admiral and Rear-Admiral similarly referring to the two next officers in command, who were all officially styled Captains.

Lord High Admiral

1360

Sir John de Beauchamp was first appointed as such.

1369

Admirals of the North and West were appointed, at the same time that Sir Ralph Sigurnell held the office of 'Lord High Admiral and Constable of Dover Castle and Lord Warden of the Cinque Ports.' It appears that the King decided to divide up the Lord High Admiral's powers.

1391
Edward of York, Earl of Rutland and Duke of Albermarle, was appointed Admiral of the North, and later became Admiral of both fleets with the title of Admiral of England.

1412
Beaufort, Earl of Dorset, was appointed as Admiral of England, Ireland and Aquitaine.

The title was regularly held till 1628, when the assassination of Buckingham brought the line temporarily to an end, and a Commission of six was formed to carry on the office of Lord High Admiral.

1638
Charles I, anxious to obtain the political support of the Duke of Northumberland, who had been Admiral of the Ship Money Fleet of 1636 and 1637, appointed him Lord High Admiral during pleasure, and not for life as the former Lord High Admiral had been appointed, and took care to make it known that a patent appointing his son, Prince James (then five years old), as the future Lord High Admiral had been prepared.

March 1642
Political tension between the King and Parliament came to a head, and, on Northumberland obeying the request of the Commons to appoint their nominee to command the fleet in opposition to that of the King's, the latter revoked the Duke's patent as Lord High Admiral.

A Board of Admiralty, consisting of seven Commissioners, was then appointed; Northumberland was, however, shortly afterwards reinstated in his former office.

1643
The Earl of Warwick was made Lord High Admiral, and continued as such till 1645, when he resigned, but was again called to office for a year from 1648.

In 1649 the office of Lord High Admiral was abolished, and the power vested in a Council of State, many of the powers being transferred to a committee known as the Commissioners for the Admiralty and Navy.

1660
Charles II nominated his brother James, Duke of York, as Lord High Admiral, the Commission for the Admiralty

and Navy being dissolved, Pepys taking over their office and papers. James's patent created him Lord High Admiral of England, Ireland and Wales, including the long lost Calais, Normandy, Gascony and Aquitaine.

A subsequent patent made him High Admiral of Dunkirk, New England, Jamaica and numerous other places abroad, including 'Guinny, Binny and Tangier.'

1673

James resigned his offices, but retained the Admiralship of Scotland (which till 1707 had a separate Admiralty) and the High Admiralship of all the places mentioned in his second patent.

A Board for executing the office of Lord High Admiral of England was then constituted, with Prince Rupert at the head, the King reserving the emoluments of the Lord High Admiral and also the appointment of officers.

Most of the important business was transacted by the King with the assistance of Pepys.

1679

James had to leave the country and a new Board was formed, which succeeded in wresting from the King the whole of the High Admiral's patronage.

1684

Charles II threw over the Admiralty Board, and resumed the powers, with Pepys as secretary. James, on succeeding to the throne, continued this arrangement.

1689

King James having fled the country, Pepys ran the Navy, taking his orders from the Council of Peers and William III. Commissioners of the Admiralty were appointed in March 1689, when Pepys retired from the secretaryship.

1702

Political dissensions decided the King, William III, to dismiss the Board of Admiralty and to appoint the Earl of Pembroke as Lord High Admiral.

William III died on March 8th, 1702, and Queen Anne appointed her husband, Prince George of Denmark, in place of Pembroke. The legislative Union with Scotland in 1707 altered the title of Lord Admiral to that of High Admiral of Great Britain.

A FIRST RATE MAN of WAR, taken from the DOCKYARD PLYMOUTH.

1708
The Prince Consort died October 28th, 1708, and the Queen acted as Lord High Admiral until November 29th, when the Earl of Pembroke was reappointed. A year later, however, on November 8th, 1709, the Admiralty was

again placed in commission, and remained without disturbance for over one hundred years.

1827
Admiral of the Fleet the Duke of Clarence (afterwards William IV) joined the Administration as Lord High Admiral with a Council to His Royal Highness in place of the former Admiralty Board.

1828
This departure lasted till September 17th, when the office was once more placed in the hands of Lord Commissioners, and has so remained ever since.

Vice-Admiral of the United Kingdom

The office of Vice-Admiral of the United Kingdom is a survival of the ancient office of Lieutenant-Admiral, or Lieutenant of the Admiralty.

The Lieutenant-Admiral first comes into view as the deputy or assistant of the High Admiral about 1350.

The title was altered to Vice-Admiral of England in 1672, then 'of Great Britain' in 1707, and 'of the United Kingdom' in 1801.

From 1876 the office was dormant till 1901, when it was revived by King Edward VII, and has been continuously held ever since.

Rear-Admiral of the United Kingdom

Charles II appointed his natural son Henry, Duke of Grafton, then only a child, Vice-Admiral of England, and probably, in view of his tender years, created Admiral Arthur Herbert 'Rear-Admiral of England.'

The office was variously held till the death of Sir William Fanshawe Martin in 1895, when it lay dormant till 1901, being revived by King Edward VII, and has been held continuously ever since.

Up till 1870 salaries were attached to the offices of Lieutenant-Admiral, etc., but in this year it was decided that the emoluments would cease after the next vacancies.

Affigraphy, fitted to an

Denotes a perfect fit.

Aiguillette (*see* Uniform)

The aiguillette is now only an ornament, and its origin is somewhat uncertain.

An aguillette

Several traditions account for the origin, some saying that they denote the rope and pegs which the squire carried wherewith to picket his knight's horse: others that the aiguillettes were 'aiguilles,' or needles used for clearing the touch-holes of the old muskets, with the lanyards which fastened them to the soldier's accoutrements. It is even suggested that they were the Provost Marshal's rope with which he hung malefactors. It is possible that they were merely exaggerations of the bunches of ribbons which were the earliest form of epaulette.

All standing, to be brought up

Unexpectedly stopped, also used to denote when, in a conversation, an entirely unlooked-for remark is made. Expression derived from sailing ship days when a ship under way was stopped without previous preparation.

Anchors

From the Greek word for a hook or crook.

The most ancient anchors consisted of large stones, baskets full of stones, sacks filled with sand, or logs of wood loaded with lead, such anchors being used by the ancient Greeks.

Later an anchor with one arm was invented, and later still one with a second arm. The anchor then resembled those in modern use, except that the stock was absent.

The largest anchor was the sheet-anchor, and only used as a last resource.

1813
A clerk in Plymouth yard, named Pering, introduced curved arms for the anchor.

1852
The Admiralty pattern anchor was supplied to ships, followed by the Rodgers anchor, in which the arms were in one piece, and pivoted at the crown. This anchor was very well thought of, and was placed second only to the Trotman anchor.

Later came the 'Martin's' anchor, self-canting and close stowing.

1894
The improved Martin Adelphi pattern anchor of cast steel was introduced.

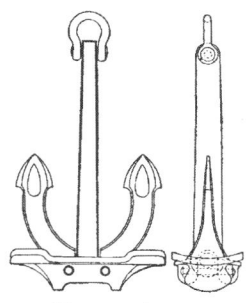

Stockless anchor

All the above-mentioned anchors had stocks.

1903

Stockless anchors were introduced into the Royal Navy.

It is surprising to find how few and how small were the anchors before the eighteenth century. A first-rate ship of 1,700 tons was allowed three anchors of 430, 150, and 174 lbs. A second-rate ship was allowed three anchors of 315, 110, and 72 lbs., while a third-rate ship was allowed three anchors of 173, 96, and 68 lbs.

WEIGHING ANCHOR.

The ship of that period must have held the wind to a far greater extent than a modern ship, taking into consideration the heavy spars and high freeboard which then existed, and yet her anchors were ridiculously small in proportion to those carried by a modern ship of similar tonnage.

Andrew Miller

An expression used on the lower deck for 'The Royal Navy.'

Apron

The apron protects the leadsman's clothing from damage when heaving the lead.

Articles of war

'The law relating to the government of the Navy, whereon, under the good Providence of God, the wealth, safety, and strength of the kingdom chiefly depend.'

The Articles of War are founded on a book, now at the Admiralty, known as the Black Book. This book contains some ordinances previous to the reign of Edward III, but there is no writing therein prior to the reign of Henry VI. Towards the end of the eighteenth century the Black Book disappeared, and no one seemed to know anything about it. There was, however, a modern transcript of the Black Book in the Admiralty Library, and there were various documents and manuscripts in the British Museum. These were collated, and it was thus possible to enable the text of the Black Book to be restored with reasonable accuracy by 1871.

In the interim there was also found an English manuscript in the library of the College of Advocates in the Doctor's Commons which was entitled *An abstract of our laws of Oleron and of the Ancient Black Book*. This manuscript was not available after 1858, as the library of the College of Advocates was dispersed and sold.

In 1874 the original Black Book was found at the bottom of a chest supposed to contain the private papers belonging to a former Advocate Registrar of the Admiralty Court.

The Laws of Oleron

The Laws of Oleron, on which the Black Book was based, were accepted by all the seafaring nations of the West, and were a code adopted, according to tradition, in Castile by Alphonso X in the thirteenth century, and during the reign in England of Edward II.

In support of the tradition it may be stated that the Island of Oleron furnished an important contingent of the fleet which set forth in the second year of the reign of Richard I to relieve the Holy Land. Among the five Commanders of this Fleet was William de Fory of Oleron, whom Richard I appointed as one of the justiciaries of his Navy.

The Code was based on some old sea laws formulated in the Republic of Rhodes, and received and conformed to by the Romans and all the States bordering on the Mediterranean.

The jurisdiction of the Admiralty was defined in the time of Richard II in the following terms: 'Admirals and their deputies should confine their jurisdiction to things done upon the sea, and in great ships being and hovering in the main stream of great rivers, yet only below bridges of the same rivers, nigh the sea.'

The provisions of the Code of Oleron included the following:

- Anybody who committed a murder at sea was to be bound to the corpse and buried alive with it.
- Theft on board was treated with boiling tar and feathers.
- Sleeping on watch was punished with dipping in the sea.
- When the Captain wished to discharge the crew, he was to give them notice of his intention by taking away the tablecloth three meals in succession.
- In certain circumstances the Captain was always to consult the crew and act according to the majority, as, for instance, whether the weather was suitable for sailing. If the Captain went to sea against the advice of the majority of the crew, he was to make good any damage to ship or cargo.

Avast

Probably the word 'fast' with the prefix 'a', meaning 'on.' Thus avast means 'hold fast' or 'stand fast.'

Aye, aye

The word 'aye' is old English for 'yes.'

Ballads

A few examples are given:

The best cry we like to hear
On board, as I'm a sinner,
Is when from the quarterdeck they call
To the boatswain to pipe to dinner.

One night came on a hurricane, the sea was mountains rolling,
When Barney Buntline turned his quid and said to Billy Bowline,
"A strong sou'-wester's blowing, Billy, can't you hear it roar now?
Lord help 'em, how I pities all unhappy folks on shore now."

A sailor's life's a pleasant life,
He freely roams from shore to shore;
In every port he finds a wife,
What can a sailor wish for more!

The girl who fain would choose a mate
Should ne'er in fondness fail her,
May thank her lucky stars if fate
Should splice her to a sailor.

A rhyme by the side party of the *Hercules* hung up in the side party's mess on Christmas Day, 1873:

Remember the side party, if you please,
As polishes the side of the Hercules,
What made the Shah exclaim as he passed down the line,
"Oh, Lord! how the sides of that ship do shine!"

Ballast

This used to be called 'pig ballast' when made of lead, and 'sow ballast' when made of iron.

Balza raft or copper punt

This is so called from the 'balza' tree from which such rafts were made.

The tree produces a spongy wood which is very light, and the raft was made of five, seven or nine logs of this wood.

Banyan days

The Banyan Days in the old Navy were Monday, Wednesday and Friday.

The Banians were a class of Hindu merchants who, being of the Vaisya caste, abstained from the use of meat. Ships on the East Indian Station probably adopted the word to signify the days on which no meat ration was issued, plum duff being served in lieu, and the expression became general throughout the Navy.

The meat ration was so bad that the meatless day was looked forward to, and so in time the Banyan Day became associated with occasions of feasting and plenty. To-day the words are included in the bluejacket's vocabulary and signify a day of rejoicing, an enjoyable outing or pleasant event.

Beef chit

Slang name for a menu.

Bighi Naval Hospital (see Malta)

Bitter end

From the *Seaman's Grammar*, 1653, Chapter VII: 'A bitter end is but the turn of a cable about the bits, and veare it out little and little, and the bitter's end is that part of the cable doth stay within board.'

Black dog for white monkey

An expression to mean something for nothing. The word 'Rabbits' is also used with the same significance.

Bluejacket

The seamen of the Royal Navy obtained this name from the only jacket which was made uniform for them. It consisted of a short jacket, much like a boy's Eton jacket, and was similar to those now worn by boys of Greenwich Hospital School.

Blue lights, old

The gunner of a ship.

Blue Peter

Blue Peter

In the Navy it has been used as a recall signal since 1777, when it was known as the flag 'blue pierced with white'; and the term Blue Peter flag, which is met with some twenty-five years later, is probably a corruption for blue-pierced flag. In sailing-ships days, when convoys were weather-bound for long periods and held up also by embargoes on sailings during wartime, passengers would reside on shore till the signal to repair on board was displayed by the escorting man-of-war. The naval blue-pierced flag was in consequence the one signal that everybody using the sea knew when they saw it; and its corruption from blue-pierced to Blue Peter is readily understandable. An autograph poem, signed Emma, from Lady Hamilton to Lord Nelson, written when Nelson sailed for the Baltic in 1801, is entitled "Blue Peter," and begins:

Silent grief and sad forebodings
(Lest I ne'er should see him more)
Fill my heart when gallant Nelson
Hoists Blue Peter *at the fore.*

It is sometimes stated that the word 'Peter' is a corruption of the French word '*Partir*,' 'to leave,' but no authority for this statement can be found.

Boats

In the reign of Edward III, 1327–1377, we read of the 'grete boat' alias 'long boat,' and the 'cokke.' The great boat rowed forty oars, and the cokke twenty.

1495
A boat called a 'joliwat' (hence our 'jolly boat') is mentioned, rowing ten oars.

1603
The 'cock boat' is still mentioned.

1624
The 'cockswain' or 'cockson,' as the steersman of the 'cock,' is defined by N. Bailey as 'An officer of a ship, who takes care of the cockboat, barge or shallop, with all its furniture, and is in readiness with his crew to man the boat upon all occasions.'

In 1634 the 'cockson' was the lowest of the four officers entitled to use and wear silver whistles, the others being the Captain, Master, and Boatswain.

1626
Long boats, pinnaces and jolly-wats are spoken of.
The long boat was 51 feet long, 4 feet beam.
The jolly-wat was 19 feet long, 5 feet 4 inches beam.
The pinnace was 28 feet long, 7 feet beam.

Mention was also made of a shallop and a barge.

1509–1660
Writing of these times, Oppenheim says 'As has been customary for at least one hundred and fifty years, each ship possesses three boats, a long boat, pinnace and skiff.' Davits are not mentioned.

The 'long boat' was apparently still towed astern.

1634
Ships carried a long boat, skiff or shallop and a barge.

Long boat	Was hoisted inboard, fitted with a davit over the bows for laying out or weighing the anchor.
Skiff or shallop	Used for ship's work.
Barge	'Served for state and ease (As for carrying the Generall Admiralls and Prynce Captains).' It was essentially the Admiral's boat, rowing ten to twelve oars.
Pinnace	Term derived from the Spanish '*pinaza*,' and this again from the pinewood of which it was built for lightness and speed.

PORTSMOUTH POINT.

1630
Was in common use as a man-of-war's boat, and rowed eight oars.

1750
Blanckley says: 'All ships are allowed one for the use of the Commander.'

Gig and galley

The clincher built gig came in as a substitute for the Captain's boat with the nineteenth century.

The 1815 edition of Falconer's *Dictionary of the Marine* calls it 'A long narrow boat … generally rowing six to eight oars, and is mostly the private property of the Captain, or Commander.'

Galley

The term is not older than 1850, and at the date of the Crimean War was exclusively applied to the boat of a Captain of a line of battleship, but the term has never been officially recognized by the Admiralty.

Dinghey

The word is derived from India, and was copied from the East India Company's Service.

A 'dinghy' is mentioned as having been supplied to a ship in 1831.

The 'yawl' is mentioned as the smallest boat supplied to a ship in 1750, only rowing six oars.

Cutters

1769
Falconer says of them: 'Cutters of a ship are broader, deeper and shorter than the barges and pinnaces.'

1804
They are spoken of as carried, hoisted to davits, on the quarters of H.M.S. *Venerable*.

Boatswain

Derived from 'boat' and 'swain,' a servant.

Boatswain's pipe or call, the

The four parts are:

- The buoy
- The keel
- The gun
- The shackle

For further details of the calls, etc., see the article by Lieutenant J. F. Ford Anderson, in *The Mariner's Mirror*, Vol. I., p. 9.

Bombardier

The title was originally that of the man who looked after the 'bombard' or 'mortar.'

Bone, to

Means to steal. Said to be derived from a Lieutenant Bone who was convicted of theft in the beginning of the nineteenth century.

Boom, top your

Addressed to an unwanted person, means 'Go away.'

Bow

This was an early name for shoulder.

Bowse, to

To pull upon a body with a tackle or complication of tackles in order to secure or remove it.

Bowse, to put in the

To be put in the report (defaulters). To get into trouble.

Bridle

Term used in cable-work. The short length of cable from the bows of a ship to the buoy.

Broad arrow

Palliser's *Historic Devices, Badges and War Cries*, published in 1870, contains the following explanation:

'The "Pheon" or barbed fishing-spear was considered as a badge of Royalty as early as the reign of Richard I, and under the name of "Broad R" (either a corruption of broad arrow, or an abbreviation of Rex) is the Royal Mark affixed to the Naval Stores in the Dockyards.'

The Broad Arrow on the reverse of a military watch

Another explanation is that the broad arrow was the seal of Lord de L'Isle, who was the first Commissioner of Ordnance in the reign of Queen Elizabeth, and was used to mark Government stores.

The *Broad Arrow*, a defunct military periodical, states in an article that this symbol is derived from an ancient Cymric sign called the three rods or rays of divine light, which signified the radiating eye of divine intelligence shed upon the Druidic circle. This symbol is said to have conveyed the sense of holiness and royalty.

The same article records that the symbol was adopted by Edward III, the Black Prince, and other Princes of Wales.

The following instances of the broad arrow being used to mark Crown property in ancient times are also on record:

In 1536, according to records of the City of London, a man was convicted for improperly marking certain barrels of ale with an 'Arreive hede,' alleging they were the property of the King.

In 1553 and the year following it was employed by Sir Thomas Gresham as a mark for gunpowder and specie shipped to England for the Crown.

In 1598 the mark was employed by the Collector of Customs at Newcastle for contraband goods which he had seized.

1687

James II, in his charter to the Tower of London, speaks of the broad arrow which 'By his late Majesty's special command (i.e. Charles II) had been set up, as His Majesty's mark, upon all the boundary houses.'

1698

Act of Parliament, 9 and 10 William III, cap. 41; 'An act for the better preventing the imbezlement of His Majesty's stores of war,' forbids the marking of goods with the broad arrow, by stamp, brand or otherwise, except for Government stores.

Bugle

The badge worn by Rifle and Infantry Regiments is the ancient form of the bugle.

Bugle is a French word; it originally meant 'wild ox,' and the real expression was 'bugle horn,' i.e. 'wild ox horn.'

The bugle was the horn of the chase, and in the fourteenth century the horn signals were most elaborate.

The bugle calls were written by Joseph Haydn, the great musician, about 1793, and were introduced into the Navy in 1865. The first buglers in the Navy came from the Royal Marines, but in 1870 instructions were given to train a certain number of boys annually.

The number of calls in 1865 were 20; in 1901, 60, and in 1928, 59.

Bugtrap

Name given to small gunboats.

Bumboat

A boat employed to carry provisions, vegetables and small merchandise for sale to ships.

One derivation accounts for the term as corrupted from 'bombard,' the receptacle in which beer is carried to soldiers on duty. Another derivation states that the word comes from, 'bum' or buttocks, on account of their clumsiness, or perhaps from 'boom,' such boats being allowed to lie at the booms of anchored ships.

Bundle man

A married man — and was so called from the permission granted him by the Service to carry a portion of his allowance of fresh provisions ashore: which he did tied up in a coloured handkerchief, as he went over the side on leave.

To be 'bundled' is to be married.

Burgee

A very doubtful derivation states that the word was formerly 'budgee,' derived from the town of Bougie, near Algiers.

Canvas

From 'cannabis,' hemp. Formerly numbered from 1 to 8, No. 1 being the coarsest.

Capsize

To upset. This is derived from the Spanish word '*cabeza*,' meaning head, and up to a hundred years ago was looked upon as very vulgar slang.

Capstan

It is said to have been invented by Sir Samuel Morland, who died in 1695, but the probability is that he only improved the then existing device. The first element of the word is from the Latin '*capere*,' to take hold of.

Captain

In the eleventh century the ship was usually commanded by the 'Batsuen' (Boatswain), or by a higher officer, the 'Rector,' in which case the Batsuen steered the ship. The rank of Captain came into use about 1370, the rank was higher than that of Master, who sailed the ship, and the former drew double the pay, two shillings a day.

Possibly the Captains commanded a division of the fleet. In the sixteenth and seventeenth centuries there were two categories of Captains, one consisting of men who were true seamen and worked their way up, and the other of men who entered the Service and had risen by interest.

In an Order in Council of February 10th, 1748, settling relative rank with the Army, Captains were divided into three classes:

1. Captains commanding post-ships, after three years from the date of their first commission for a post-ship.
2. All other Captains commanding post-ships.
3. Captains of ships or vessels not taking post.

All ships down to 6th rates (24 guns) were post-ships. Every officer commanding a vessel had the title of Captain, though his rank were but lieutenant.

Post-Captains appeared in the *Sea Officers List* (the forerunner of the *Navy List*) with P against their names; Captains not taking post were styled Masters

A Post-Captain

and Commanders and had C against their names for Commander.

The rank of 'Master and Commander' was not shortened to Commander in the official lists till 1794, and the change from P for Post-Captain to C for Captain, and from C for commander to Cdr did not take place till 1826.

The rank of Post-Captain signified that the officer's name was posted or included in the list of Captains eligible for promotion to the rank of Rear-Admiral.

Careen

The word is derived from the Latin word '*carina*,' meaning a keel.

Blanckley's *Naval Expositor* (1750) gives the following:

'A ship is said to be brought on a careen, when the most part of her lading, etc., being taken out, she is laid alongside the hulk, which, being lower than her, is hauled down as low as occasion requires, in order to trim her bottom, to caulk her seams, or to mend anything that is at fault under water.'

Cartridge paper

In Tudor times the charges for medium and small guns were made up in paper cases, hence the early application of this term.

Cashier

The term is derived from the Dutch '*casseeren*,' having the same meaning as the French '*casser*' – to break. In its original sense, however, it did not necessarily imply disgrace.

Caulk, to take a

This term, which is descriptive of 'Taking a nap,' is derived from the fact that when sleeping on the deck one's back becomes marked by the pitch from the seams.

Chains

In a sailing ship the shrouds are attached to a platform on the ship's side, and in practice the bottom part of these were of chain. The platform was in consequence called the 'chains,' and used for heaving the lead. Now, although the position of the platform for the leadsman is altered, the name still remains the same.

Chain cables

Up till 1811 cables were made of hemp and were twenty-one inches in circumference. In 1811 chain cables were introduced.

It is interesting to note that chain cables were in use in the Mediterranean 1,000 years before they were introduced into the British Navy.

Chair, a bosun's

A short piece of wood to form a seat, fitted with a rope sling. With the latter bent to a rope a man can be triced up for work on the mast.

Chaplains

It has been customary to carry chaplains in ships from early days, one chaplain being carried for each division of the Fleet, while in the reign of Charles I a chaplain was appointed to each ship in the Fleet.

Pay and duties. – Both chaplains and doctors used to be paid by the seamen: each seaman had to pay the chaplain fourpence a month and the doctor twopence a month.

Prayers were read twice a day, and every time the watch was changed either a psalm or hymn was sung. The chaplain was also authorised to reward any midshipman who learned a psalm with sixpence.

Messing arrangements. – Up to the end of the eighteenth century he did not necessarily live in the wardroom. For a long time the wardroom was a mess for the lieutenants only, though the master was usually a member. The chaplain, purser and doctor usually messed in their cabins; but sometimes the chaplain messed with the captain. It may also be noted here that Marine officers were ordered in 1671 to mess with the Captain.

Marryat's ex-Lieutenant Chaplain. – Marryat mentions a chaplain who had been a lieutenant prior to changing his rating and taking Holy Orders. He was an excellent chaplain, but, as he had also been a very zealous and capable lieutenant, he was apt in an emergency, such as a gale of wind or action, to forget his Holy Orders, and to take charge as a lieutenant, exhorting the seamen in language less suitable to a chaplain than a lieutenant. After one of these occasions, a midshipman discovered him dissolved in tears and stricken with remorse at the recollection of the language he had used. The midshipman consoled the chaplain by assuring him that he was mistaken in thinking he had damned the men, and further assured him that the only words he had been heard to utter were 'God bless you, my men! God bless you!' For this act the chaplain rewarded the midshipman with a bottle of rum.

Charley Moore

There was an expression 'Come, now! That ain't the Charley Moore,' meaning that it was underhand. Perhaps he was the Charles Moore who served in the Mediterranean in the latter part of the Napoleonic War, and was promoted Commander while in the *Royal Sovereign* yacht, for heroic intrepidity in rescuing the crew of a French vessel driven on shore off Calais.

In 1905 there was a public house in Valetta, Malta, called 'Charley Moore, the Fair Thing.' The sign was done up by the late Admiral of the Fleet Sir Edward Seymour.

Charlie Noble

This is the name for the galley (cook-house) funnel.

Charlie Noble is said to have been the commander of a line of battleship, and was the first man to have the galley funnel polished.

The term has now died out, but can be traced back for a hundred years.

Chest at Chatham, the

This was founded immediately after the Spanish Armada by Sir John Hawkins, Treasurer of the Navy, assisted by Drake and others in 1590.

The origin of the Chest at Chatham arose out of the consideration 'that by frequent employment by sea for the defence of this Kingdom ... divers and sundry Masters,

Mariners, shipwrights and seafaring men, by reason of hurts and maims received in the Service, are driven into great poverty, extremity and want, to their great discouragement.' It was therefore voluntarily agreed that every man and boy in the Navy and the Merchant Navy should regularly forfeit to the fund a proportion of his monthly wages, such contributions to be, from time to time, placed in a strong chest with five locks to that purpose specially provided.

The Chest, which is of iron, still exists in the Royal Naval Museum, at Greenwich, where it was placed by the Admiralty in 1846.

Not till 1829 did the stoppage on behalf of it, of sixpence each month from the wages of every seaman in the Royal Navy and Merchant Service, cease.

Although the idea of a fund was an excellent one, yet in actual practice the history of the management of the fund is very sorry reading.

Choke the luff, to

To place suddenly the fall of a tackle close to the block, across the jaw of the next turn of the rope in the block, so as to prevent the leading part from rendering.

Christmas

The decoration of the ship on Christmas day, the rounds of the mess-decks by the officers, the wearing of petty officers' rig by the boys, and so on, are believed to be a survival of the Roman custom; this was that, during this festival, the masters took the places of, and waited on, their own servants.

Chum, a long-haired

Described a friend of the female sex in the days when ladies wore long hair.

Clean-boiled rag, a

A white starch-fronted shirt.

Clean in a dirty rig, to

To change into a dirty suit or refitting rig.

A Chip of the Old block

Clean in the rig of the day, to

To change into the dress ordered for the day.

Clinch, out to a

Used in cable-work when the cable is out to the full extent. In conversation it means that everything possible has been done.

Cobbing

A beating or caning.

The *Oxford English Dictionary* gives one meaning of to cob as to fight, give blows.

Falconer's *Marine Dictionary* (1769):

'Cobbing. A punishment sometimes inflicted at sea. It is performed by striking the offender a certain number of times on the breech with a flat piece of wood called the cobbing board. It is chiefly used as a punishment to those who quit their station during the period of the night watch.'

Cobbing

Cock a chest, to

To be pleased with oneself.

Cockbill

The situation of an anchor when suspended from the cat-head. To put the yards 'a-cockbill' is to set them aslant. A symbol of mourning.

Coming up, one for

An extra pull to allow for taking a turn with a rope. Used in conversation to mean an extra.

Commander

Before 1827 the Commander (originally 'Master and Commander') was employed only in command of a small ship of war of less than 24 guns, a sloop of war, armed vessel or bomb vessel. The title came over with William III as 'Commandeur,' and was simplified from 'Master and Commander' to 'Commander' in 1794.

Commanders were first appointed as seconds in command of big ships in 1827, an innovation which the Navy at first disliked, but when the three Commanders of the *Asia, Genoa* and *Albion*, after the battle of Navarino, were, at the expiration of a year from the date of their appointments, promoted to the rank of Captain, and made Companions of the Bath with three foreign decorations, the appointments were eagerly sought after.

For 'Master and Commander' see also under CAPTAIN.

Commissions, length of, about 1811

The following commissions are recorded:

H.M.S. *Centurion*. Eleven years in the East Indies.

H.M.S. *Rattlesnake*. Fourteen years, and finally returned home with only one man who was in the original crew.

H.M.S. *Fox*. Fifteen years. During the whole of this long commission not one farthing was paid to the crew.

Commodore

The title of Commodore originated with the Dutch at the outbreak of the Dutch Wars in 1652, when, owing to the lack of Admirals in the Dutch Navy, and a reluctance to create more, the title was introduced, and was brought over to England by William III. The broad pendant burgee (or budgee) of the Commodore was introduced by the Dutch at the same time as the title. The rank was not officially recognised until 1806.

Cont line

The space between the bilges of two casks stowed side by side.

Cookery

Terms used to describe dishes:

Acting rabbit pie	Bacon and beef made into a pie and baked.
Bangers	Sausages.

Burgoo	Another name for porridge. Formerly a dish made of boiled oatmeal, seasoned with salt, butter and sugar.
Burnt offering	Any roasted meat. Also described as a lazy cook's dinner, consisting of the meat ration as drawn from the beef block, placed in a dish, and surrounded by potatoes, then baked. The name is derived from the condition in which it usually arrives at the table.
Deep sea beef	Salt beef. Also used as a term to describe haddocks.
Dog's body	Dried peas boiled in a cloth.
Dog's breakfast, a	A mess.
Dough boys	Formerly hard dumplings boiled in salt water, a corruption of 'dough balls.' Now used as a general term for dumplings.
Figgy duff	Raisin pudding.
Hoosh-my-goosh	A stew.
March past, a	Meat placed on pudding, and baked in a dish.
One-eyed steak	A bloater.
Schooner on the Rocks	Roast meat on potatoes, or a joint baked in batter.
Soft tack	Bread ration as opposed to the hard biscuit.
Spithead pheasant	A kipper.
Steerage ammick	Pork, currants and raisins laid up in a pudding, lashed up in a cloth representing a hammock and then boiled.
Three decker, a	Slices of beef, divided with layers of suet pudding to the number of decks required, and the whole boiled in a pot.
Tin of sharks, a	A tin of sardines.
Underground fruit	Vegetables.
Yankee hash	Beef, tomatoes, etc., cut up and stewed.

Copper sheathing

This was introduced into the Navy from 1760 to 1820.

Coxswain

See under BOATS.

Craft

From the Anglo-Saxon '*craeft,*' a small trading-vessel.

Crowfoot

A number of small lines spreading from an 'uvrow' or long block, used to suspend awnings by.

Also a kind of stand, attached to the end of the mess-tables, and hooked to the beam above.

Crusher

Ship's police.

Cuddy

A sort of cabin or cook-room, generally in the fore part, but sometimes near the stern of lighters and barges of burden.

In the Oceanic traders it is a cabin abaft, under the round-house or poop-deck, for the Commander and his passengers. Also a little cabin of a boat (Smyth's *Sailor's Word Book*). Now used to denote the Captain's cabin.

Crummy

Dirty.

Cumshaw

In general terms means something extra, or thrown in, not bargained for. Derived from the Chinese for grateful thanks.

Customs of courtesy, etc.

All these have a reason, either of courtesy, sentiment or utility, or a combination of the three.

Many customs in practice are not confined to the Service, but are universal to all who use the 'seas.' Some of these are:

- One ship standing by another in distress.
- Women and children abandoning ship first.
- Captain leaving a sinking ship last.
- Merchant ships dipping to a man-of-war.

Other customs more or less confined to the Service include the following:

A man-of-war commanded by a junior officer lying at anchor, on the approach of a ship commanded by a senior officer, asks permission to get under way so as to leave the anchorage clear for the senior to anchor in whatever billet he desires.

Respect is shown to an Admiral or senior officer when met at sea, even if he is not in command of the squadron to which the ship belongs, by asking his permission to proceed before parting company.

The custom of showing courtesy by juniors getting into a boat first and out last is an unwritten one: in a seaway the last man in and the first man out gets the shortest period of bucketing.

A jealously guarded tradition is that of the Royal Navy and Royal Marines being allowed to march through the streets of London with bands playing, colours flying and bayonets fixed: only three Regiments of the Army have this privilege, namely the Grenadier Guards, the East Kent Regiment (The Buffs) and the Royal Fusiliers (City of London Regiment). In the case of the Royal Marines the origin of the privilege is possibly due to the fact that the Marines were recruited from the 'trained Bands of London,' when certain of these bands were disembodied in 1664. When the Royal Navy gained the privilege is not known.

The 'Attention' is sounded on the bugle when one man-of-war passes another, because, from the earliest times, ships have saluted one another when meeting, in order to indicate their mutual esteem.

A ship is 'manned' for similar reasons, and to accentuate the feelings of respect shown. This also has been done from the earliest times; first the shrouds were manned, then the yards, and in these days the upper deck.

The coat of arms of The Buffs

A ship is 'dressed' with flags to commemorate an occasion, or to show joy or respect at some great personage's presence.

A junior officer commanding a ship asks permission before crossing the bows of a ship commanded by his senior in rank.

Cut and run

This is derived from the practice in the old days of using yarns instead of gaskets when furling the sails: the yarns could be cut and sails let run.

Davits

For hoisting boats were introduced some time between the years 1790 and 1804.

Deadman, a

A yarn or rope's end hanging untidily from a spar.

Dead marine

Applied to an empty bottle, as having done its duty, and ready to do it again.

Derrick

It is said that the name is derived from Thomas Derrick, a well-known hangman of the time of Queen Elizabeth and James I.

Devil to pay

The expression was originally 'The devil to pay and only half a bucket of pitch.'

The 'Devil' was a very large, important and difficult seam of the ship to caulk, and half a bucket of pitch would be totally inadequate to 'pay' it. (*See* PAY.)

Dish, trim the

To right the balance of a boat to an even keel.

Ditch, to (an article)

To throw overboard.

Ditty-box

A ditty-box

A small caddy for holding a seaman's stock of valuables (Smyth's *Sailor's Word Book*).

The same authority gives the derivation of 'ditty' as from 'dittis,' a Manchester stuff of which the 'ditty-bag' was once made.

The *Oxford Dictionary*, however, states that there is no evidence of this, nor is anything known of the stuff alleged.

Doctors

Hauls off the Scottish Coast. – Apparently most of the doctors in the Navy came from Scotland. During the seventeenth and eighteenth centuries the principal exports from Scotland were said to be 'birch' brooms and doctors. It is also said that when the Navy was short of doctors a frigate would be sent to cruise inshore off the Scottish coast: whenever a group of natives was observed standing on the beach, a jolly-boat, filled with porridge, would be veered astern till it touched the beach. The natives would crowd into the boat after the porridge and then the jolly-boat would be hauled off to the ship, and would always be found to be full of doctors.

An unkind medical yarn. – A great many unkind stories have been told about the naval doctors of the past. One story relates how a certain doctor always kept down the number of men on the sick list by the following method: every morning he would enter the sick bay and in stentorian tones would order the sick-bay steward to bring him his knife with the long curved blade. At the sound of this order the vast majority of the men who were awaiting outside the sick bay would glide swiftly and silently away.

Economy in medical appliances. – The naval doctors of the seventeenth and eighteenth centuries were always complaining of the inferior drugs and appliances with which they were supplied. At one time naval hospitals were ordered to use sponges instead of lint for dressing wounds, the former being considered more economical as they could be used over and over again. This economy vastly increased the number of cases of blood-poisoning.

The wounded in action. – It was the custom at one time to attend the wounded in the order in which they arrived in the cock-pit, irrespective of either their rank or injuries. This custom appears at first extremely democratic, but it often led to a badly wounded man bleeding to death, while a man who had been wounded earlier in the action, but whose wounds were less serious, was being attended to by the doctors.

Dodging Pompey

Getting out of a job by a subterfuge.

Dog watch

A corruption of dock watch, i.e. a watch which was docked, shortened.

Doggy

A midshipman A.D.C.

Dog's body

Used as a term of belittlement.
Also *see* under COOKERY.

Donkey

Term applied to the small black chest used by carpenters and other artisans in which to carry their tools.

Donkey's breakfast

A term signifying a straw mattress.

Dose from the foretopmen's bottle, a

Term used by the sick-berth staff to signify a dose of white mixture.

Doss, to have a

Doss is a corruption of the French word '*dos*', meaning back, and thus lying down is interpreted as 'having a doss.'

Douse

To lower or slacken down suddenly. To 'douse' a light is to extinguish it.

Drums

They were an Oriental invention, and were brought back from the Crusades.

Dusty boy

A member of the victualling staff.

Ensign

Royal Navy ensign

Corruptly written 'ancient' during the sixteenth to eighteenth centuries.

This word was borrowed from the land Service in the sixteenth century, to denote the striped flag then introduced on the poop of vessels.

Barret, who wrote *The Theorike and Practike of Moderne Warres* in 1598, states, in explaining the meaning of this word in the army: 'We Englishmen do call them [Ensigns] of late, "Colours," by reason of the variety of colours they be made of, whereby they be the better noted and known to the companie.'

ENSIGN, shortened from Ensign-bearer, became a rank in the land Service, and was adopted as a naval rank in the French Service.

In 1862 the United States Navy adopted the rank of Ensign to denote passed Midshipman, following the change in the British Navy, where the rank of Sub-lieutenant had been adopted in April 1861 in lieu of the previous rank of Mate.

Epaulettes

These were originally bunches of ribbon, and were simply for ornamental purposes.

See UNIFORM.

Euphroe (uvrow)

A circular piece of wood with holes in it, by which the legs of a crowfoot are extended for suspending an awning.

Eyes of the ship

The early ships had a monster's head or other symbolical figure carved in the bows of the ships, and the fore part was then called the 'head': it is therefore natural that the eyes should go with it, and hence we speak of the 'eyes of the ship.'

Fair do-es

Slang for justice or fair treatment.

Fair wind, a

In an officers' mess one is not asked to pass anything, it is e.g. 'Give the salt a fair wind.' If a dish is passed by hand at table, and the person to whom it is passed helps himself from it without taking the dish in his own hands, the person passing it is at liberty to drop the dish and the receiver pays for it if broken.

Fanny Adams

A name given to tinned meat in the Royal Navy. A history of the lady can be found in a chap-book published between 1805 and 1815 entitled *The love, joy and distress of the beautiful and virtuous Miss Fanny Adams, who was trapann'd into a false marriage*, etc. Another chap-book, called *The life, trial, sentence and execution of Frederick Baker of Winchester for the murder of Fanny Adams*, shows that Baker was a solicitor's clerk who not only killed the girl, but cut up the body and disposed of the pieces in the river near Alton. The case was naturally much spoken of, and probably some wag of a sailor applied the name to the pieces of salt meat which were at that time served out to the Fleet. It is said that the meat was often so old and hard that tobacco boxes were made out of it and that these took a fine polish!

As a matter of fact, Fanny Adams lived and died thirty years or so before the first contract for tinned meat was made with a Mr. Goldner of Galatz, Roumania, in 1844. The quality of the goods he supplied was atrocious, horses' hoofs and even shoes being said to have been found in the tins.

The Merchant Navy adopted tinned meat much later, and favoured another nickname, 'Sarah Lane', or 'Harriet Lane,' derived from a somewhat similar case.

Feu de Joie

Since the Sovereign is the symbolic head of the Army, it is natural that joy should be shown on the occasion of his birthday. Noise has been, from time immemorial, a means of paying high honour and of expressing joy: the Oriental still beats drums or discharges firearms and fireworks on the occasion of a wedding or other 'feast.'

The Feu de Joie, where each man fires his rifle in turn, is a more personal and striking method of expressing pleasure than volleys, and incidentally it also prolongs the noise. The Prince of Orange is credited with being the originator of the practice after the taking of the fortress of Wesel in 1629.

The drill was curious: an equal number of pikemen and musketeers were drawn up in line, each pike having a wisp of straw fastened to its point and every musket being loaded with powder only. The straw was set alight, and each musketeer in turn tried to blow out the wisp opposite to him by discharging his piece. The pikes were 18 feet long, so it followed that the muskets would be pointed upwards. This was an almost exact counterpart of our modern Feu de Joie.

The chronicler says: 'The volley met with a stop at first, as was perhaps natural at the first attempt, but eventually it ran well.'

Fiddles

A wooden framework placed on a table to prevent plates, glasses, etc. rolling off.

Flags

Origin of the pennant, Commodore's burgee and Admirals' flags.

The commonly believed origin of the pennant which is worn at the masthead of His Majesty's ships in commission is as follows: On November 30th in the year 1652 Admiral van Tromp, a Dutchman, with a fleet of 80 ships and 300 merchantmen encountered Admiral Blake in the Straits of Dover and worsted him. It was after this victory that van Tromp is said to have sailed up the Channel with a broom at the masthead as a sign that he had swept the British from the face of the seas. Admiral Blake is supposed to have hoisted a whip at the masthead of his ship as a sign that he would whip the Dutch into submission. He carried out his threat, and we are sometimes told that the present pennant was carried ever afterwards in memory of Blake's whip.

This theory is, however, not borne out by history. The pennant came into use long before the time of Admiral Blake; it dates certainly from the thirteenth century, when seamen were mere nobodies, when there were no such things as regular men-of-war, and ordinary merchantmen were either hired or commandeered for use as fighting vessels whenever the necessity arose. These requisitioned ships were commanded by military officers, gentlemen in armour, who, on embarking, transferred their single trail pennons, borne on their lances, to the mastheads of the ships.

In larger ships or squadrons there was the likelihood that the Commanders would be Knights or Knight Bannerets, and they flew their swallow-tailed or square banners whenever they risked themselves afloat.

It is possible that these emblems have been handed down to posterity as the Captain's pennant, the Commodore's burgee, and the Admiral's flag of the present day.

Admirals' flags

Previous to 1634 there was rarely more than one Admiral in a fleet who flew the St. George's flag or the Royal Standard at the masthead.

1634
When three-masted vessels were common, the Admiral flew his flag in the maintop, the Vice-Admiral in the foretop, and the 'Rere Admiral' in the 'missen top,' with the crosses or colours of their nation and countrymen. This also obtained for fleets of merchantmen.

1625
Squadronal colours were introduced, the Admiral's squadron wearing red flags, the Vice-Admiral's blue, and the Rear-Admiral's white.

The Admirals' flags were worn at the main, fore and mizzen mastheads respectively.

The Admiral commanding in chief, although he was not a Lord High Admiral, wore the Royal Standard at the main. Normally the Senior Admiral wore the Union flag at the main, the other two Admirals wore the Union flag at the fore and mizzen respectively.

1653

The order of seniority in colour of the flags was changed to red, white and blue.

1702

Hitherto the white colours consisted of:

1. A plain white flag for the Admiral.
2. A plain white ensign with a small St. George's cross in the upper canton near the staff.
3. A plain white pendant with a St. George's cross at the head.

The white Admiral's flag was replaced by the Union flag, the white ensign by a red one with a broad white horizontal stripe through it.

The reason for this change was that, at this time, the French flag was white.

The Admiral's boat-flags were distinguished by the use of white balls, two for a Rear-Admiral, and one for a Vice-Admiral.

Later in the same year the white ensign was reintroduced instead of the red ensign for ships on the white Admiral's squadron, with a very broad red St. George's cross in it.

The boat-flags of the Vice- and Rear-Admirals of the White were again changed, the colour of the balls being altered to blue.

1805

The rank of Admiral of the Red was introduced.

1864

The division of Flag Officers into three categories was abolished, the white colours being retained for the Navy. Red balls were substituted for the blue balls in the boat-flags.

1898

The invention of the modern battleship with only two masts, one of which was often unsuitable for the display of a flag, led to the adoption by Vice- and Rear-Admirals of the boat form of the flag, and though the question of a suitable flag for Vice- and Rear-Admirals was raised in 1898, it was thought advisable to continue this method, but, to make the flags more easily distinguished, the balls were increased in size, and the second ball placed in the lower canton.

Senior officer's pendant

1684
A red swallow-tailed pendant with a large cross at the head was instituted by Lord Dartmouth, then in command of an expedition against Algiers.

1686
The use of this pendant was kept up, though not officially recognised.

The pendant appears to have been very broad and short, with a red swallow-tailed fly, and a blue saltire surmounted by a red cross on a white ground at the head.

1692
The use of a Senior's pendant seems to have spread, and was put down by an Admiralty order.

1864
A small broad pendant, white with the St. George's cross, was ordered by the Admiralty.

Masthead pendant

1623
Pendants were merely a means of beautifying a ship.

1633
Pendants used to distinguish ships of the various squadrons.

1661
In addition to the red, white and blue squadronal pendants, there was a fourth with the fly striped red, white and blue, used to distinguish H.M. ships in commission which did not form part of a fleet divided into squadrons.

The first step towards the recognition of the pendant as the distinctive sign of a man-of-war was taken by the Proclamation of 1661, which assigned the Union Pendant to H.M. ships only, and the next by the Proclamation of 1674, which forbade merchantmen to fly any pendant whatsoever.

1824

A pendant, white with a red St. George's cross, with a fly either red, white and blue or entirely of the colour of the particular ensign worn by the ship.

In modern times the pendant is white with a red St. George's cross in the head.

Paying-off pendant Is not officially recognised, but it has been the practice for more than one hundred years and was in use during the Napoleonic war. A crippled ship returning from Trafalgar wore one.

Commodore's broad pendant

1674

A red swallow-tailed pendant was approved to be worn by the officer in command of ships lying in the Downs, though not a flag officer.

1676

Pendant altered to white swallow-tailed with a red St. George's cross.

1806

The rank of Commodore officially recognised, and a broad pendant of squadronal colour laid down as the official pendant of that rank.

The pendant carried a white ball if the Commodore had no second Captain in the ship.

1824

Commodores were divided into two classes, the first class flying the red or white pendant, and the second class the blue pendant.

1864

Squadronal colours were abolished and Commodores of the first class ordered to wear the white swallow-tailed pendant at the main, and those of the second class at the fore.

Later, the Commodores second class adopted the red ball in the upper canton of the burgee.

St. George's cross as the English national flag Little is known of the life of St. George, except that he was a soldier who attained the crown of martyrdom during the reign of Decius, about the year 250.

St. George was a soldier's saint and not a churchman's, and attained his popularity amongst the Crusaders, men

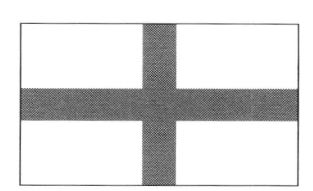

English flag

who did not reverence saints and knew the names of very few.

Why a red cross on a white field came to be associated with St. George is not known.

The cross of St. George was probably first adopted as the English national symbol by Edward I, being used for the pennoncels on the spears of the foot soldiers, and for the 'bracers' which the archers wore on their left forearms.

About 1348

St. George was recognised as the patron saint of England. The Chapel of St. George was founded at Windsor in 1348.

1574

Ensigns first appear amongst sea stores.

It seems probable that from the fourteenth century onwards ships not belonging to the King or to the nobility flew the flag of St. George, when they flew any flag at all.

By the end of the sixteenth century the flag of St. George had taken the lead as the distinguishing characteristic of English ships, both men-of-war and merchantmen.

The Union jack

Union jack

The Union flag (though not then so called) took its rise from a Proclamation issued by James I on April 12th, 1606, when, baulked of his desire to unite the realms of England and Scotland in one, he strove for a lesser degree of union under one common flag.

The Proclamation decreed that from henceforth 'All our subjects … shall bear in their maintop the red cross commonly called St. George's cross, and the white cross called St. Andrew's cross joined together according to the form made by our heralds, and sent by us to our Admirals to be published to our subjects, each nation retaining their own flag in the foretop.'

The new flag, however, pleased neither nation.

Although the Proclamation did not differentiate between men-of-war and merchantmen, a distinction appears to have been made by the addition, in the case of Royal ships, of a 'jack' (i.e. a flag flown on the bowsprit) and a pendant.

1634

The Union flag was reserved 'As an ornament proper for our own ships (men-of-war) and ships in our immediate service and pay.'

1649

The execution of Charles I dissolved the dynastic union between England and Scotland, the two nations fell apart, and the Council of State abolished the Union flag, and ordered the English ships to revert to the old English flag of St. George.

Later on in the same year a new Union flag was decided on for Naval use, this time embodying the Union of England and Ireland.

1658

The Union jack (England and Scotland) was reintroduced with the addition of the 'Harpe.'

1660

The 'Harpe' was removed, 'it being offensive to the King.'

Union flag with harp

1661

A Proclamation specifies flags, jacks and pendants, this being the earliest use of the word 'jack' as distinct from 'flag.'

1801

Owing to the legislative union with Ireland the flag was altered to the appearance it presents to-day.

(The only authoritative work on naval flags is *British Flags*, by W. S. Perrin [Admiralty Librarian], published by the Cambridge University Press, 1922. I am greatly indebted to Mr. Perrin for permission to use his book.)

Fleet up, to

To move along, generally used when sitting in a row.

Fore and aft rig

In a sailing ship means any vessel not square rigged, i.e. without yards.

A fore and aft rig in a man means that he is not dressed as a seaman in jumper and blue collar but as a petty officer with blue coat and brass buttons.

Forecastle

This term came into use in the twelfth century, when castles, similar to the war buildings on shore, were added both fore and aft to Norman ships.

A survival of the nomenclature of 'after castle' is found in the manner in which the gear of the quarterdeckmen is marked, namely 'AX,' as opposed to that of the forecastlemen, which is marked 'FX.' It has survived probably because it is much easier to cut AX with a Service knife than QD (quarterdeck).

Foretopman's crest, a

A patch on the seat of the trousers.

Fox

A fastening formed by twisting several rope yarns together by hand, and rubbing it down with hard tarred canvas. Used for a seizing, or to weave a paunch or mat.

Full due, for a

An absolute finishing; an unchangeable decision.

Funeral exercises

In the funeral exercises there remains some remarkable symbolism in the shape of the reversed arms, the three volleys fired in the name of the Trinity (which custom has been traced back as far as Sir Philip Sidney's funeral), and the Last Post. The significance of the high ascending note on which the latter ends is one of hope and expectancy.

Stephen Graham, who served for some time as a private in the Guards, writes very appositely: 'When a soldier dies, the Union Jack is laid upon his body in token that he died in the Service of the State, and that the State takes the responsibility for what it ordered him to do as a soldier.

'The reversed arms are an acknowledgment of the shame of killing. Death puts the rifle to shame, and the reversal of the barrel is a fitting sign of reverence.

'The three volleys fired into the air are fired at imaginary devils which might get into men's hearts at such a moment as the burial of a comrade-in-arms. An old superstition has it that the doors of men's hearts stand ajar at such times and devils might easily get in.

'The Last Post is the Nunc Dimittis of the dead soldier. It is the last bugle call … but it gives promise of reveille … of the great réveillé which ultimately the Archangel Gabriel will blow.'

Funny party, the

Slang name for a ship's concert party.

Galley (cookroom)

The origin of the term is unknown.

Defined as a place in the cookroom, where the grates are set up and in which they make fires for 'boyling or roasting the victuals.'

1758
The cookroom was in the hold of the ship.

1816
It was recommended to move the cookroom to the forecastle.

Gashings

Remnants.

Gibby, a

A tablespoon.

Gilguy

A cunning device or apparatus.

Gobby

Expression used for a man belonging to the old coastguard service. 'Gobby ships' were the ships of the Reserve Fleet Stationed, as was the custom for many years, at the chief non-naval ports of the United Kingdom.

Greenwich Hospital

(*Including the Painted Hall and the Royal Naval Museum*)

Henry V granted the Manor of Greenwich to Thomas Beaufort, Duke of Gloucester, for life. The property later passed to Humphrey, Duke of Gloucester, youngest son of Henry IV, who was granted permission to enclose 200 acres of land, and later to build a house, which he called 'Placentia.'

The house stood near to the river at the north-east part of the grounds of Greenwich Hospital.

At Humphrey's death the property reverted to the Crown, and it became an important Royal residence. Here Henry VIII, and his children Queen Mary and Queen Elizabeth, were born. King Edward VI died here in 1553.

At the Restoration, Charles II found the buildings beyond repair, and they were all pulled down except the 'Queen's House,' which it was decided to incorporate in a new building from designs by Inigo Jones.

The new building was unfinished when William and Mary allocated it for a Seamen's Hospital in 1694.

The building erected by Charles II forms the eastern half of the north-west quarter of the present buildings. The western front erected in 1696–1698 was rebuilt in 1814.

The three other quarters are called:
- Queen Anne's building, commenced in 1698.
- King William's building, commenced between 1698 and 1703.
- Queen Mary's building (in which is the chapel) was finished in 1752.

The general design for the completion of the buildings was from the plan of Sir Christopher Wren.

The funds for the building and maintenance of the hospital were derived from the King, from grants made by Parliament, gifts by private individuals, and a duty of sixpence per month paid from the wages of the seamen. Money collected from fines paid by smugglers, from unclaimed prize money and money from estates forfeited to the Crown were also paid into the funds for the upkeep and maintenance of Greenwich Hospital.

The property of 'The Chest at Chatham' was also transferred to Greenwich Hospital.

Greenwich Naval Hospital

Pensioners were first received in 1705, and in 1814 reached a total of 2,710 men, besides out-pensioners.

In 1865 the administration was vested in the Admiralty.

As time went on the number of pensioners decreased, until in 1869 all the pensioners were given out-pensions and ceased to live at the hospital.

The buildings, with the exception of the infirmary, which was lent to the Seamen's Hospital Society in lieu of the *Dreadnought* Hospital Ship, remained unoccupied up to 1873, when they were devoted to the purposes of a Royal Naval College, which purpose they fulfil to-day.

The Royal Hospital School

Founded in 1712 for the purpose of educating the children of the pensioners.

The school is now devoted to the education of the sons of warrant officers, petty officers and men of the Royal Navy, Royal Marines, men of the Royal Naval Reserve and other seafaring persons.

The boys have to enter into an agreement to engage for continuous service in the Royal Navy from the age of eighteen years.

Thanks to the generosity of Mr. G. S. Reade of New Zealand, the Royal Hospital School is to be moved to more suitable quarters at Holbrook (near Shotley), in Suffolk.

Painted Hall

Built as a banqueting-hall or refectory for the pensioners from the designs of Sir Christopher Wren, and finished in 1703.

Formerly the officers dined in the upper chamber and the pensioners in the lower. As time went on the number of pensioners increased, the table of the officers was discontinued, and other dining-rooms for the men were provided in the basement.

The Painted Hall was then left unoccupied for many years, until in 1823 it was utilised as a picture gallery to house a 'National Gallery of Marine Paintings to commemorate the eminent services of the Royal Navy of England.'

The painting is by Sir James Thornhill, and took twenty years to complete.

Here in 1806 the body of Lord Nelson lay in state prior to the burial in St. Paul's Cathedral.

A Greenwich Pensioner, 1828

Queen's House

Built as a residence for King James I by Inigo Jones. During the Civil Wars, Councils of State were held here, and under its roof Admiral Blake lay in state.

In the plague year it became the Navy Office.

From 1829 to 1841, in connection with the Royal Hospital School, the building was used as a girls' school, since when it has been used to accommodate the officers attached to the Royal Hospital School.

In 1927 the Admiralty granted the use of the 'Queen's House' as a national Naval and Nautical Museum, a shrine worthy to house the nautical treasures of the British Empire.

For further information see Professor Callender's historical sketch in the *Annual Report* (1929) *of the Society for Nautical Research.*

Queen's House

Grenade

This word is derived from the Spanish *granada*, meaning pomegranate, the original grenades being made in that shape.

Greyhound lash-up, a

A lashed-up hammock, with little bedding inside it, lean and lanky.

Grog

Beer was originally the ration, one gallon being the daily issue; this ration was very necessary, as the water on board was, as a rule, undrinkable, and until the beginning of the nineteenth century there was neither tea nor cocoa. It was almost impossible to keep the beer good when at sea, and, as Lord Howard wrote to the Admiralty in 1588, 'Nothing doth displease the seamen so as sour beer.'

In the seventeenth century wine, instead of beer, was issued to ships going to the Mediterranean.

Rum crept into use, and prior to 1740 a ration of a neat half-pint was served out each morning and evening, a quantity which was often doubled if the weather was unusually severe. In 1740, however, Admiral Vernon prohibited the serving of neat rum, and ordered it to be diluted, before issue, with water.

Pouring rum

Admiral Vernon was known as 'Old Grog,' owing to his custom of wearing a 'grogram' cloak (grogram is a coarse material made of silk and mohair. Name derived from gros-grain).

In 1824 the half-pint ration was reduced to one gill, and tea was issued in lieu of the other gill.

In 1881 the issue to officers, other than warrant officers, was stopped. Before then, any commissioned officer could take up as many bottles of rum as he chose, from the paymaster, at a shilling the bottle.

The toast on the grog-tub is 'The King, God bless him,' and the reason therefor is that originally the ship's company assembled round the grog-tub, and drank the King's health.

Grow, to

How does the cable grow? i.e. in what direction does the cable lead from the hawsepipes. The cable officer indicates the direction by pointing.

Guess, or guest rope

A rope carried to a distant object, in order to warp a vessel towards it, or to make fast a boat (Smyth's *Sailor's Word Book*).

Gun, son of a

A certain number of sailors were, at one time, allowed to keep their wives on board, and the expression 'son of a gun' signified the children who were actually born on board under the berthing of a broadside gun.

Gunroom

The Gunroom owes its name to the fact that it was originally the store-room and mess of the gunner and his mates. Midshipmen, on first coming to sea, were placed under the charge of the gunner for instruction. There was a midshipmen's berth, but only the seniors lived therein, and the younger midshipmen messed in the flat outside.

As a consequence, these younger officers got into the habit of using the gunner's room, and as time went on the midshipmen's berth disappeared, and the gunroom

The Interior of a Midshipman's Berth, 1821

became the home of the subordinate officers, but no longer that of the gunner.

The gunroom as a mess place for the junior officers was officially so called in 1853.

See WARDROOM.

Guns

First mentioned in English naval records in 1338, when three cannon with chambers and a hand gun figured amongst the stores of *The Christopher of the Tower* ('of the Tower' signified that the vessel belonged to the Sovereign).

Guns were not in common use, however, in the Navy till several years later, and are not frequently mentioned till about 1373.

Hammocks

On October 19th, 1492, Christopher Columbus landed at Exuma in the Bahamas, where he found that the natives used as beds, nets of cotton stretched between two posts, which they called '*Hamacs*.'

This word was changed into '*Hamaca*' and '*hamaco*' by the Spaniards, under which name it entered the English nautical vocabulary in the reign of Queen Elizabeth.

In 1596 hammocks are first officially mentioned in the Navy as 'hanging cabbons' or 'beddes.' Later on they were called 'hamackes' and 'hamackoes,' and were always made of a brown canvas until well into the nineteenth century. A ship prided herself more on the whiteness of her hammock-cloths than on the appearance of her hammocks. After an action every effort was made to expend more sails than were actually damaged by the enemy's fire, so as to get new canvas for hammock-cloths, and also new white trousers for the ship's company.

In 1653 Generals Deane and Monk wrote to the Admiralty Commissioners from on board the *Resolution* as follows:

'There will also be wanting a considerable number of hamacoes, there being about 3,000 men in the Fleet, at this time, lying on the decks for want of them, as the Captains of Vice-Admiral Penn's fleet informs us, which breeds great disturbance amongst the seamen and we know not how to answer them.'

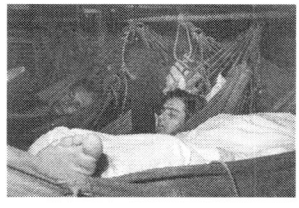

Sailors sleeping in hammocks

The expressions 'Up hammocks' and 'Down hammocks' are due to the old practice of having the hammocks stowed in nettings on the upper deck. In the days of Nelson it was a common jibe at the French that they could not even give the orders correctly for getting the hammocks up and down, for they said 'up' when slinging, and 'down' when stowing.

To give a man 'time to sling his hammock' means to give him time, on joining a ship, to look round and to settle down.

Hand: lend a hand or bear a hand

'Lend a hand' is a request for assistance, as opposed to 'Bear a hand,' which is more in the nature of an order.

Handsomely

Order meaning 'slowly,' 'with care.'

Hard a-gilbert

Hard a-port. Origin unknown.

Hardtack

The name for biscuit.

Haslar Hospital

The land was purchased in 1745, and the building completed in 1762 from the designs of Mr. John Turner, who modelled his plans on those of Greenwich Palace, designed for King Charles II by Inigo Jones.

In the early days of Haslar, the medical officers were civilians who were allowed to add to their meagre salaries by private practice, to the detriment of their official duties, but in 1797 an order was issued forbidding private practice.

John Howard, the prison reformer, visited Haslar in 1788, and reported as follows:

'All the nurses are women, which is very proper, as they are more cleanly and tender; and they more easily pacify the patients who are seafaring men.'

Apparently they did not always succeed in pacifying the men, for one Nurse Olaye complained of 'having been beaten by a patient,' and in 1798 another nurse was nearly beaten to death! Also with reference to John Howard's visit and referring to the rules respecting ventilation in the wards:

'In the fever, flux, and small pox wards, a small chink of the upper part of some one or more of the windows is constantly left open, so as at night gently to move the flame of a candle standing on the table, unless otherwise ordered by the physician.'

Hawsepipes

Hawse is an early name for throat, and, as the fore part of the ship was known as the 'head,' it naturally followed that the name 'hawse' should come into use.

Holiday, a

A space between two objects.

Holy stones

The larger ones are called 'hand-bibles' and the smaller 'prayer-books.'

So called because when using them an attitude of prayer is taken up.

Holy-stoning the deck

Hour and half-hour glasses

Even as late as 1857, half-hour and hour glasses were used in the Navy for the purpose of keeping the time.

House a mast, to

To lower it, taking care that, when housed, the rigging is not resting or chafing on the cap.

The heel is secured to the mast below.

Idlers

Falconer's *Marine Dictionary* (revised 1815) gives 'Idlers' as a general term for 'all those on board a ship of war who, from being liable to constant day duty, are not subjected to keep night watch, but nevertheless must go upon deck if all hands are called during the night.'

The term is used to-day to mean cooks, shipwrights, sickberth staff, etc., and does not accurately express their activities, as they work extremely hard.

Jackshalloo

This is in all probability derived from a naval character, John Chellew, who was notorious for his noisy recklessness.

Chellew is a West Country name.

Jag up, to

Old rope is put up, or 'jagged up,' for returning to store in five-fathom lengths.

Jaunty

This name for the Master-at-Arms is a corruption of the French *gendarme*.

Jelly belly, a

A name for a fat sailor.

Jew, the

The ship's tailor.

'Jewing' is the term used to denote the making of clothes on board.

Jimmy Bungs

A nickname for the cooper.

Joss, good or bad

Signifies luck, good or bad. Derived from the Chinese word for an idol.

Junk

Was the old name for condemned rope, and was also used to mean salt beef, as the latter was so stringy.

Kedge

From the old English word for 'brisk.'
Kedge-anchors were usually run in to a quick step.

Killick

A term for an anchor.
Also a slang term for a 'leading seaman.'

Knife, purser's

This knife had no point, with a view to avoiding hasty stabbing cases, and also so as to cause less injury when dropped from aloft.

Lammy suit

A suit made of thick fearnought, or blanket, for night wear.

Lance

The word 'lance' in Lance-Corporal or Lance-Sergeant of Marines means 'lance' in a literal sense. In old days mounted men were considered superior to those on foot; a mounted man-at-arms might be, and often was, unhorsed during a battle, being then compelled to fight with the foot soldiers, but the lance which he still carried would indicate his former rank and gave him a certain prestige. From the 'Lance man of the Foot,' as he was then called, we get our modern lance ranks.

Larboard

This was the term formerly used to denote the opposite side of the ship to starboard (steerboard), and was so called from the 'load-board' or loading-plank being placed on that side; the ship was naturally placed alongside on the opposite side to the steerboard in order to prevent any damage to the latter. Owing to frequent mistakes larboard was changed to port or loading entrance.
See under PORT.

Launching a ship

The breaking of a bottle when a ship is launched originated with the practice of drinking prosperity to the ship out of a silver cup, which was then thrown overboard.

This practice continued up till 1690, but, being found too expensive, the breaking of a bottle on the bows was instituted.

Up till 1811 the ceremony was always performed by either a Royal personage or one of the Dockyard Commissioners, but in that year the Prince Regent introduced the custom of ladies performing the ceremony.

On one occasion a lady, who was performing the ceremony, made a bad shot with the bottle, hitting and injuring a spectator, who sued for damages. As a consequence the Admiralty directed that, in the future, the bottle should be secured by a lanyard to the bows.

Libraries on board ship

Libraries were introduced on board ships in 1812, and a few of the books supplied were *The Old Chaplain's Farewell Letter*, *Wilson's Maxims*, *The Whole Duty of Man*, *Seeker's Duties of the Sick* and Gibson's *Advice After Sickness*.

Lick and a promise

Means anything done perfunctorily.

Lieutenant

From the French signifying 'one who replaces' or a substitute.

A rank introduced in 1580 with the intention of providing the Captain of a ship with an executive assistant qualified to take his place on an occasion.

Lizard

A rope on the lowerbooms for securing boats to.

Loggerheads

These were heavy iron bars which were heated and then used to melt the pitch for caulking.

Long ship, a

It is obvious that in an argument they proved to be most useful weapons.

An inhospitable ship in which there was a long while between drinks.

The story is told of a visit paid by the Kaiser to a British man-of-war, when he tactfully said, 'This is a long ship, is it not,' and was told, in all seriousness, by her Captain the actual dimensions of the vessel!

Lurgees

To have an attack of the 'lurgees' is to be shirking one's job.

Mafeesh

Expression signifying finish. Derived from the Maltese.

Malta

Royal Hospital, Bighi The original naval hospital was the old slave prison at the bottom of Strada Cristoforo, which continued in use till 1822, when the hospital was transferred to the Armoury at Vittoriosa, and at the same time the grounds at Bighi were transferred to the Navy for the purposes of a hospital.

The promontory on which Bighi Hospital stands is the Monte Salvatore, so named from the little church close by the main gates of the hospital.

This church was destroyed during the siege, and rebuilt in 1580. The original building on Monte Salvatore was erected as a country house, 'Villa Bighi,' by the Italian knight, Fra Giovanni Bichi (or Bighi).

In 1803 the Villa Bighi was officially reported on as a suitable spot for a naval hospital, but it was not till 1832 that the naval hospital was transferred from Vittoriosa to its present site.

Royal Hospital, Bighi

Marines, Royal

The first corps raised for sea service of which history gives an account, is that which was formed by King

Charles II in the year 1664, when the war with Holland took place: this corps was commanded by the Duke of York (afterwards James II), then Lord High Admiral of Great Britain, and was designated *The Admiral's Maritime Regiment*.

'By Order-in-Council, dated October 26th, 1664, it was directed that twelve hundred land-soldiers should be raised, in order to be in readiness for distribution in His Majesty's fleets; the whole to form one regiment, of six companies, under a Colonel ... each company consisted of two hundred soldiers. ...

'A subsequent Order-in-Council, dated 1st April 1668, authorised the drawing of such numbers of soldiers from the Foot Guards for His Majesty's service at sea, during the summer, as the Lord High Admiral might require' (Cannon's *Historical Record of the Marine Corps*, p. 1).

... 'It is supposed that the regiment was very largely recruited from the London trained bands, and it is considered to be due to this fact that the present corps of Royal Marines enjoys the privilege of marching through the City of London with bayonets fixed, colours flying, and drums beating. (Another reason has been suggested for the privilege, i.e. that it originated from Warrants issued by Charles II to the Marines and other regiments who share it, authorising them to raise recruits "by beat of drum" within the precincts of the City of London.) This privilege is shared with the 3rd Battalion Grenadier Guards, the East Kent Regiment (the Buffs), and the Royal London Militia, all of which were originally recruited from the same source. This privilege since 1915 has been extended to the 1st and 2nd battalions of the Grenadiers, but the companies now forming the 3rd Battalion are considered especially to represent those which fought afloat in the Dutch War – and to this day "Rule Britannia" is played before "The King" at Tattoo, in commemoration of its Marine service. Major Donkin (in *Military Collections and Remarks*, New York, 1777) related that in 1746, as a detachment of Marines was beating along Cheapside, one of the magistrates came up to the officer requiring him to cease the drum, as no soldiers were allowed to interrupt the civil repose. The Captain commanding said: "We are Marines." "Oh, sir," replied the Alderman, "I beg pardon. I did not know it. Pray continue your route as you please." The descent of the corps from the trained bands is also commemorated by the universal nickname "Jolly" for a Marine. "Tame Jolly" was an old cant name for the citizen soldiers; and according to Admiral Smyth's *Sailor's Word Book* "Royal Jolly" was a time-honoured phrase for a Marine in contradistinction to the "Tame Jollies" or Militiamen' (*Britain's Sea Soldiers: A History of the Royal Marines*, by Colonel Cyril Field, R.M.L.I., 1924, Vol. I., p. 17).

In the 3rd Dutch War (1672–1674) 'several companies of the Foot Guards were employed on the Marine duty' (Cannon's *Historical Record of the Marine Corps*, p. 2).

'In 1689 King William III incorporated "The Admiral's Regiment" (which was then considered the third regiment of Infantry) in the second, now the Coldstream, regiment of Foot Guards' (Cannon, p. 2).

'Two Marine regiments were, about the same time (i.e. 1689), established for service on board the fleet, which were disbanded in 1698 (i.e. following upon the Treaty of Ryswick, when the fleet was demobilised) (Cannon, p. 2).

'On the recommencement of hostilities, in 1702 ... six regiments were accordingly added to the regular Army as *Marine Corps*; and six other of the regular regiments of Infantry were appointed for *sea service*;

'The six Regiments of Marines were the (in 1830) 30th Foot, 31st Foot and 32nd Foot; and 3 regiments disbanded in 1713.

'The six Regiments for sea service were the (in 1830) 6th, 19th, 20th, 34th, 35th and 36th Foot.

'... Other regiments were also embarked, at different periods during the war, on board the fleet to act as Marines ... The Marine forces were placed under the command of the Lord High Admiral (H.R.H. Prince George of Denmark). ... When the Marines were serving afloat they were to be under the command of the naval officers of the ships. ...

'During the reign of Queen Anne certain Independent Companies of Marines were raised for the ... defence of the British possessions in the West Indies. ...

'Peace was restored by the Treaty of Utrecht on 31st March, 1713. ... The corps of Marines were ordered to be disbanded. ... The establishment of the regiments of infantry were increased, and in consideration of the gallant and extensive services of the Marine corps during the late War, Colonel Wills' (now 30th Foot), Goring's (now 31st Foot) and Borr's (now 32nd Foot) were incorporated with the regiments of infantry of the line, and ranked according to the dates of their original formation in 1702 (Cannon, p. 21).

'War was formally declared against Spain, 23rd October, 1739. ... Orders were issued for augmenting the land-forces, and also for forming *six regiments of marines*; the Colonel Commanding the First Regiment of Marines was Colonel Edward Wolfe, from the 3rd Foot Guards and his son, James Wolfe, received his first commission (dated 3rd November, 1741) in his father's regiment (though he exchanged into the 12th Foot on 25 March, 1742). In 1740 *four additional* regiments of Marines were raised (making 10 in all); also an additional regiment, of four battalions, was authorised to be raised in America, and the royal standard was erected at New York, as the signal post to which every volunteer Marine was to repair. The field officers and subalterns were appointed by the King, and the Captains of companies were appointed by the American provinces. Colonel Spotswood, of Virginia, was appointed colonel-commandant of the whole. ...

'By Royal Warrant, dated 28th February, 1746/7, i.e. 1747, the entire command of the Marine corps was placed under the Admiralty. Upon the Peace of Aix-la-Chapelle in October 1748 the *ten regiments* of Marines were disbanded.

'On the recommencement of hostilities with France in 1755, fifty companies of Marines were raised, under the direction and control of the Admiralty. These companies were formed into three divisions, at the principal naval stations, Portsmouth, Plymouth, and Chatham (a fourth division was formed at Woolwich in 1805). The *Carps of Marines* having been raised in 1755, and since that period retained on the establishment, as a branch of the permanent national force ... have been authorised to rank, when acting with Infantry of the Line, next to the 49th Regiment (by Horse Guards General Order, dated 30th March, 1820).

'On 29th April, 1802, the day of the Proclamation of Peace which ended the war of the French Revolution, the King signified his approbation to Lord St. Vincent,

Royal marine private in 1815

then First Lord of the Admiralty, "that the Corps shall in future be styled the Royal Marines" in order to mark the King's approbation of the conduct of the Corps during the past war.

'On 26th September, 1827, the Duke of Clarence (Lord High Admiral) presented new Colours to the Chatham Division of the Royal Marines, and in the course of his speech said:

'"His Majesty (i.e. George IV) has selected for the Royal Marines a *Device,* to which their achievements have entitled them, and which, by his permission, I this day present to you:

'"*A Badge,* which you have so hardly and honourably earned. From the difficulty of selecting any particular places to inscribe on these Standards, your Sovereign has been pleased to adopt 'The Great Globe itself,' as the most proper and distinctive badge. He has also directed, that his own name (i.e. G. R.) shall be added to that peculiar badge, THE ANCHOR, which is your distinctive bearing, in order that it may be known hereafter that George the Fourth had conferred on you the honourable and well-earned badge this day presented to you.

'"The motto, peculiarly your own: *'Per Mare per Terram,'* has been allowed to remain; and surmounting the entire is the word GIBRALTAR, in commemoration of the important services you performed there"' (Cannon, p. 48).

In June 1923 the Royal Marine Artillery and the Royal Marine Light Infantry were amalgamated.

Martello tower

So named from one erected at St. Fiorenzo at a place called Mortella, captured by the Mediterranean Fleet in 1793.

A Martello tower

Matelot

The French for sailor.

Mess, nearly to lose the number of one's

To be nearly killed.

Messmate

Companions of the same mess-table, hence comrades in many ways; whence the saying 'Messmate before shipmate, shipmate before a stranger, stranger before a dog.' (Smyth's *Sailor's Word Book*.)

Midshipman

The term originally denoted the men stationed amidships, i.e. under the Captain's eye, and were usually prime seamen. The rating of Midshipman was purely a ship's rating down to the end of the Napoleonic wars, and a Midshipman could be disrated by his commanding officer, and made to serve before the mast.

1643
The first mention of Midshipman occurs in this year, at which time it does not appear to have been a rating leading to any personal honour.

1653
It was directed that suitable men were to be selected for the rating of Midshipman, receiving extra pay; no one was to be so rated unless able, in case of necessity, to perform an officer's duties.

1676
King Charles II made regulations for the introduction of 'Gentlemen Volunteers,' or, as they were usually called, 'King's Letter Boys,' their age not to exceed sixteen years and their pay £24 a year.

1728
The system of 'King's Letter Boys' was abolished, and the Naval Academy, at Portsmouth, instituted.

1740
Admirals and officers commanding ships were allowed a great number of 'Followers,' ranging from the Admiral with fifty, to a Captain with four per hundred of complement. Some of these were rated Midshipmen, amongst the remainder figured tailors, barbers, footmen, artists and fiddlers.

A Midshipman, 1823

1794
Followers were ranged in three classes:

1. Young gentlemen, not under the age of eleven years, who were intended for the sea service, and these were styled Volunteers.
2. Boys of between fifteen and sixteen years intended to become seamen.
3. Boys of between thirteen and fifteen years intended to do actual work as servants.

It was then the common practice to bear upon the ship's books young gentlemen who were still in the nursery or at school.

Midshipman only became a naval rank after the Peace of 1815, when the number of demobilized midshipmen and the few ships commissioned made it both desirable and possible for the Admiralty to assume responsibility for their appointment.

The time borne upon the ship's books counted, of course, towards the stipulated six years' sea service, without which a boy could not be advanced to the rank of lieutenant, two years of which had to be as midshipman or mate.

The servant system remained in force till the Peace of 1815, and was the readiest means of entering the Navy.

Admiral of the Fleet Sir Provo Wallis, who died in 1894, entered the Navy in this way.

In 1779 a midshipman was hanged for murdering his mother, who had come on board his ship at Spithead, and tried to make interest with the First Lieutenant to be allowed to attend the ship as bumboat woman. The son remonstrated with her for taking such a step as calculated to lower his dignity with his brother officers. She proceeded to sit down on a chest, and poured forth on him and his wife such a stream of abuse that he, poor man, driven nearly mad, caught up a hanger and made a push at her, and unfortunately killed her.

In 1790 the oldest midshipman in the Service was a well-known character, Billy Culmer, aged thirty-five on the ship's books, but possibly much older. He occurs in Cruikshank's caricatures of naval life and eventually passed for lieutenant, going to London for the purpose, as was the custom in those days, accompanied by another

A midshipman in 1830

A Midshipman, 1828

midshipman and the boatswain to keep him sober, and a terribly hard time of it they had!

1837
The Naval College was closed, and in the same year H.M.S. *Illustrious* was stationed at Portsmouth as a cadet training ship.

1855
A similar school was opened on board H.M.S. *Implacable* at Devonport, but, as one school was soon found sufficient, the latter was closed.

1859

H.M.S. *Britannia* was stationed at Portsmouth, relieving the *Illustrious*.

1862

The *Britannia* was removed to Portland, and the following year to Dartmouth.

1869

H.M.S. *Prince of Wales* was commissioned, taking the place of the *Britannia,* was so renamed, and, linked up with the *Hindustan,* remained the officers' training establishment till September 1903, when the new system of training inaugurated by Sir John Fisher necessitated the opening of separate establishments at Osborne and Dartmouth.

April, 1921

The Osborne buildings were closed, and all the cadets concentrated at Dartmouth.

Other methods of entering the Royal Navy are from the Mercantile Marine training ships *Conway* and *Worcester*, the nautical college of *Pangbourne*, also from the South African training ship, *Botha*.

Boys are also entered from the public schools, and are trained on board H.M.S. *Erebus*.

Mooch around, to

Movements to which some sort of suspicion is attached.

Music

Naval march 'Hearts of Oak' — This should be called 'Heart of Oak,' and is a song from Garrick's *Harlequin's Invasion* of 1759. It was written and composed in commemoration of the victories of that year, namely Quiberon, Lagos and Quebec, and was a favourite in the Navy.

Royal Marine march 'A Life on the Ocean Wave' — This was written and composed in New York in 1838, the words being by Henry Epes Russell, an American, and the tune by Henry Russell, the well-known English songwriter and singer, who at that time was a young man.

Naval Crown, the

An admiral's epaulette showing the Naval Crown

The Naval Crown has a long history. The Romans awarded various 'distinctions' such as the laurel and bay leaves, mural crowns, naval crowns, etc. Their design for a Naval Crown was an interlacing of the beaks of galleys.

The British use of the Naval Crown is comparatively modern. It came into use in the seventeenth century, and may be seen in the mural tablet to Thomas Shish, Master Shipwright (died 1685), in the Church of St. Nicholas, Deptford.

It was incorporated in the arms of Greenwich Hospital, which date from William III, and its appearance on the button of the uniform of officers of the hospital may be said to be its first official use in the Naval Service.

About the middle of the eighteenth century naval officers who took out armorial bearings, or received an honourable augmentation of their arms, began regularly to incorporate a Naval Crown to show the origin of their honours. Notable examples were Sir George Pocock, Sir Charles Saunders, Sir John Jervis (afterwards Earl St. Vincent), Sir Francis Geary.

By the time of the Napoleonic War it had became the regular heraldic custom, as may be seen from Nelson's arms and those of the officers of his day. It will be seen in the arms of all the flag officers at Trafalgar: Nelson, Collingwood and Northesk.

Lord Jellicoe has also incorporated a Naval Crown in his armorial bearings; it also appears in the following cases: Greenwich Hospital Arms, Navy League badge, cap badge of the Mercantile Marine, War Graves Commission, in some ships' badges and in general use in naval establishments.

The design has never appeared on official naval medals, but has appeared on medals struck privately, namely those struck for the Brigantine *Cambrian* of 1804.

Some of the 'Promissory Naval Farthings' and similar tokens of 1794 and thereabouts have the Naval Crown thereon. Other than these, the only introduction of a Naval Crown up to Nelson's time was on a medal struck in 1692 to commemorate the battle of La Hogue.

The only later medal with a Naval Crown is that commemorating the Duke of Clarence's appointment as Lord High Admiral in 1827.

A beautiful carving of a complete Naval Crown is in the Museum of the Royal United Services Institution, surmounting the flagstaff carried by Admiral Ommaney's boat party in one of the Arctic expeditions.

The Naval Crown as usually seen is a 'half crown,' for the artists, for heraldic purposes, only draw the design as seen full face.

Naval Reserve, royal

Formed in 1859.

Navy list

The first official *Lists* were known as *Sea Officers Lists*, and consisted merely of seniority lists and alphabetical lists of officers of the executive branch.

The publication resulted from the issue of half-pay orders following on the Peace of Ryswick in 1676; the lists were issued down to 1846, when their separate publication was discontinued and the information incorporated in the *Navy List*. The *Sea Officers Lists* were for official use only, and never placed on sale to the public.

The list of 'Ships of the Navy,' with their Commanding Officers, lists of Officers of the Navy, Officials of the Admiralty, Dockyards, etc., were published annually in the *Royal Kalendar*. During the American War David Steel began the publication of his *Original and Correct List of the Royal Navy improved*, which gave the station on which ships were serving.

Steel's *Navy List* began in 1779 or 1780, and was on sale for sixpence.

Gradually Steel incorporated the information in the *Royal Kalendar* and other material, till it amounted to over fifty pages at the time of his death, in 1803, after which it was carried on under its original name on behalf of his widow.

In 1814 the Admiralty decided to place on sale a *Navy List*, the official *Sea Officers List* never having been available to the public. The *Navy List*, published by authority, was compiled in the Admiralty, and published by John Murray.

In 1868 it became a Stationery Office publication, in conformity with the procedure regulating Government publications, but continued to be published by the firm of John Murray till 1887, when the Stationery Office took over full responsibility.

On the appearance of the *Official Navy List*, with its much fuller information, Steel's *Navy List* soon ceased publication.

New Year's Eve

The custom of the youngest officer striking sixteen bells on New Year's Eve is of great antiquity, and probably the youngest officer is chosen for a similar reason to the Roman custom of reversing rank and position when celebrating Christmas.

Nicknames

Bennett	Wiggy
Bell	Daisy
Clarke	Nobby
Collins	Jumper
Green	Jimmy
Hines	Cosher
Henderson	Granny
Harding	Tosh
Harris	Chats
Long	Dodger
Martin	Pincher
Miller	Dusty
Murphy	Spud
Parker	Nosey
Sullivan	Spike
Taylor	Buck
Williams	Bungy
Woods	Slinger
White	Knocker
Ward	Sharkey
Wright	Shiner
Walker	Hookey
Wilson	Tug

Nipper

This nickname for a boy has a nautical origin, for in early days when weighing anchor the cable was not actually brought to the capstan, but an endless rope going round the capstan and forward alongside the cable was fitted; the cable was secured to this rope by 'stoppers,' known as nippers, which were worked by the boys of the ship, and thus boy becomes nipper.

Nix mangiare steps, Malta

This name was given to some steps in Valetta, Malta, by bluejackets as a consequence of the large number of beggars who used to frequent the middle of the flight of steps there and whine, 'Oh, signore! mi povero! miserabile! nix padre, nix madre, nix mangiare for sixteen days per Jesu Christo.' The sixteen days were always in English, but the statement was contradicted by the chubby faces of the children of the party.

Nobby Hewett

This is probably intended for 'Nobby Ewart,' a name given to the late Admiral Ewart, partly in approval of his neatness, and partly because of the trouble he took to beautify the part of the ship of which he had charge as mate of the main deck.

One story about him is that he ordered a dingy goose to be whitewashed, and its bill and feet to be blacked, because it was not smart enough in its coop.

Afterwards, when he went to the opera at Malta, the occupants of the gallery used to cry out, 'Who whitewashed the goose? Why, Nobby Ewart!'

Nor'-Wester, a

Not entitled. (*Note:* The expression Nor'-Easter is also used.)

Parson's Yeoman

The organ-player on Sunday.

Part brass rags, to

To fall out with your chum.

Pay

Captains' retired pay.

Up to 1747 Captains passed over for promotion to Rear-Admiral remained on the Captains' list and drew half-pay.

On the suggestion of Lord Anson in 1747, Captains were promoted to Rear-Admiral and placed on the retired list, and, as they were not commissioned as of the Blue, White or Red Squadrons, they were jokingly referred to as 'Rear-Admirals of the Yellow Squadron,' or 'Yellow Admirals.'

Paymaster

The 'clerk' or 'burser' (hence purser) appears in the fourteenth century in the King's ships, being the officer who acted as the paymaster of the crew, and who had charge of the stores and provisions.

His emoluments came more from his profits on store transactions than from his own wages; sometimes he even had to pay for his place.

1842
The title was altered to 'Paymaster and Purser.'

1852
Title altered to 'Paymaster.'

Pay to (a seam)

To pour in hot pitch after caulking to defend the oakum from the wet.

Derived from the French word '*poix*,' pitch.

Pincher Martin

Originally a nickname for the great Sir William Martin, a well-known Admiral, and indicated his smartness in discovering offenders. Sir William was also known as 'Fly' Martin, as he once commanded H.M.S. *Fly*.

Piping the side

The custom is handed down from those days when fleets were many months at sea, and commanding officers had constantly to leave their ships to visit their superiors for Councils of War, etc. At such times when the sea was too rough to permit the boats to come alongside, or when the ships were rolling heavily, it was necessary to hoist the Captain in over the nettings in a boatswain's chair by a yard and stay, and the men of course worked by pipe. Hence also the rather disrespectful remark made to the report, 'Please, sir, the Captain coming on board,' namely, 'Very well, hoist him in.'

Piquet

This term is a reminder of the days of pikes: as these were gradually superseded by firearms, a, few were still kept in the centre of the battalion as a guard for the Colours. This handful of men was known in French as the '*piquette*' or little body of pikemen, and the word was afterwards taken to refer to any small military force.

Plush

A slang name for remnants.

Poke off, to

To move away. An invitation to an unwanted person to go away.

Port

As a substitute for 'Larboard' was in use in 1580.

Post (first and last)

See under TATTOO.

Post-captain

See under CAPTAIN.

Prayers

The custom of saying prayers at sea is very ancient. In the old days it was the usage to sing hymns and psalms at the changing of the watch.

Press gang

A press gang in 1780

Originally the man who was required for the service of the King at sea was 'prest.' To prest a man meant to enlist him by means of 'prest money,' the word 'prest' being derived from the old French *'prest,'* now *'prêt,'* meaning ready.

Any man who voluntarily or under duress accepted or received the King's shilling from the recruiter's hands was said to be 'prested' or 'prest.' In other words, having taken the King's ready money, he was thenceforth during the King's pleasure 'ready' for the King's service.

In the English language there happened to be the word 'pressed,' which was almost identical in pronunciation with the French *'prest.'* Pressing men for the King's service at sea was established as an adjunct to power as early as the days of the Saxon Kings, and only died out as a means of manning the Navy as late as 1833.

In 1756, 50,000 men were sufficient for the Royal Navy; by 1780 the number required had reached 92,000, and in 1802 the total of men in actual sea pay was 129,000. Many men were required and many methods adopted to attempt to provide the increasing numbers: registration, which was adopted in 1696 for the first time, proved a failure, a system of bounty met with no better success, in fact, since it ranged from five to almost any number under one hundred pounds, it proved an irresistible cause for desertion. In 1795 the 'quota' scheme was tried, whereby every county contributed men to the Navy in proportion to its population, but this also was a failure, and eventually the Navy reverted to the press gang as a means of manning the fleet.

If It must be understood that in those times when a ship paid off the crew were dispersed ashore, being finished with the Navy. Also during the period under review, although life in the merchant service was little short of unendurable, life in the Navy was little better and the naval man lost free will, incurred additional dangers of being shot, or if he deserted was liable to be hanged. It is worthy of note that, as an example of life at sea, the old Code of Naval laws lays it down that a seaman guilty of undressing himself at sea was to be ducked three times from the yard-arm.

Continuous service was introduced in 1853.

Prique of baccy

The pigtail worn by a sailor was termed a 'prique' (possibly a nautical spelling of *perruque*), and the tobacco when made up had a somewhat similar appearance, hence the name.

Private ship, a

A ship not wearing an Admiral's flag is called a 'private ship.'

This term was used by Buckingham when issuing his instructions for the Boulogne Fleet in 1625, as follows:

'The Vice- and Rear-Admirals are to have the Union at the fore and mizen respectively, and the private ships of their squadron pendants at those mastheads.'

Promotion

From *The Times*:

Thursday, January 10, 1828. Price 7d.

Quick Promotion. – Colonel Arbuthnot, who commands the 73rd Highland Regiment, quartered at the Tower, is only 21 years of age.

Slow Promotion. – There are three Middys on board the *Victory* at Portsmouth; one is 40, another is 42, and another 45 years of age.

Pull your pound

A phrase demanding assistance in man weight, alluding to the allowance of a pound of beef daily that a man gets.

Purser's crabs

Boots or shoes issued by the paymaster.

Rabbits

See under BLACK DOG FOR WHITE MONKEY.

Raggie

A chum, i.e. one with whom you share cleaning rags.

Rat in the ship

Q. Who are entitled to keep a rat in the ship?
A. The gunnery department. The turret rat or sweeper.

Rations

The seaman's rations during the seventeenth and eighteenth centuries appear to have been very ample.

He was allowed 2 lbs of meat a day, a pound and a half of bread a day and a gallon of beer.

Savings

In order to make the stock of provisions on board last as long as possible, the sailor was nearly always on a reduced allowance while at sea. He was credited in money with the value of the balance of his allowance, and it appears to be the origin of the custom of 'Savings.'

Beer and rum

See under GROG.

Victualling

In 1622 the contractors were paid 7½d. a day in harbour, and 8d. at sea for each man fed.

In 1914 the cost price of the seaman's daily ration was only 9½d., so the contractors of 1622 must have been well paid for their trouble.

Proposed combination of Captain's and purser's duties

In the reign of Charles II the Captains of the Navy petitioned the King that pursers should be abolished and that Captains should take on the duties of purser.

The King asked, "To whom, then, should the men appeal when they think they are defrauded of their due?" The Captains replied that they would always be just.

At this the King laughed heartily, and said he was afraid that the Captains' opinions of their own honesty was not shared by everybody, and that he would sooner that things remained as they were.

The purser

The purser always appears to have been a very unpopular man, and he was in a difficult position.

Before obtaining his warrant he had to give surety for a large sum of money, and if he had not the money himself he had to rely on the contractors to give surety for him, and this put him in their power.

The Captains also sometimes insisted on a share of the purser's perquisites, which obliged the purser to invent all sorts of ways by which those perquisites might become large enough for two.

1824
Tea introduced as a ration.

1795
Cocoa introduced as a ration.

1798
Tobacco first issued.

1795
Lime-juice first issued.

Rice

Served out in 1800. The sailors hated it, and called it 'Strike me blind,' being firmly convinced that its continued use would rob them of their eyesight.

Ropes, to pull

To use influence.

Rotten row

The old expression for ships lying up in ordinary in 'routine' order.

Round house

Name derived from the semi-circular towers in the forecastle bulkheads of ships in the middle of the eighteenth century, which were used as latrines.

Round turn

To be brought up with a round turn of a rope round a bollard would suddenly check a weight being lowered.

To be brought up with a round turn in a conversa-

Rub, to ask for a

To borrow an article.

Rudder

From the Anglo-Saxon 'rother,' that which guides.

Rumbo

An expression which formerly meant rope stolen from the dockyard.

Sag, to

To bend or give way from heavy weight. To press down towards the middle.
The opposite of 'hogging.'

Salt beef squires

A term used in the old days to signify a warrant officer.

Salutes

Salutes in boats — These probably owe their origin to the custom of striking or lowering the sail, which was a mark of respect: absolutely insisted on in the case of all foreign ships when meeting a British man-of-war in what were known as the 'British Seas,' the boundaries being from Cape Finisterre to Cape Staten in Norway.

It was understood to imply an acknowledgment of the British sovereignty of these seas, and is claimed to have been exacted since the times of the Saxon Kings, but in all probability dates from the time of the Norman Conquest. In those days, lowering the sail was no empty compliment, for in ships of the period not only were they brought to a standstill by striking the big and only sail they carried, but were rendered practically defenceless as well, for the sail when lowered encumbered most of the upper deck and upper works. To strike the sail therefore placed the ship in a position in which she could easily be examined by British warships, and, if necessary, taken possession of. Hence the salute in boats of laying on oars, tossing oars, letting fly sheets and stopping engines all tend to place the boat at a disadvantage somewhat similar to that of the ship which in earlier times lowered her sail.

Salutes by raising the hand

These have their traditional origin in the custom of the tournament. The victors on appearing before the Queen of Beauty, who presided over the tournament, were accustomed to shade their eyes when receiving the prizes at her hands, the idea being that otherwise they would be blinded by her dazzling beauty. It was a very courteous and chivalrous custom, but if our modern salute is derived therefrom, then it must be by a very devious route.

The naval salute in Nelson's time was a 'touch of the forelock' – officers and men took off their hats when addressing their superiors.

It is said that the Coldstream Guards were the first to practise the modern salute, and in 1745 a regimental order ran as follows: 'The men ordered not to pull off their hats when they pass or speak to an officer, but only to clap their hands to their hats and bow as they pass by.'

A similar order was issued to the Marines in 1779.

In the Navy the salute of uncovering the head still remains, as when the Captain or Admiral inspects a division. The present naval salute was introduced in 1890.

Admiral of the Fleet Earl Mountbatten arrives on HMS Glasgow at Malta

Gun salutes

Always given in odd numbers. The reason for this custom is unknown, but is a very old one, for in *Boteler's Dialogues* (1685), published by the Navy Records Society, the matter is referred to as follows: The Captain states that the distinguished visitor to the ship 'has his farewell given him with so many guns as the ship is able to give; provided that they be always of an odd number.

'*Admiral*: And why odd?

'*Captain*: The odd number in ways of salute and ceremony is so observable at sea, that whensoever guns be given otherwise it is taken for an expression that either the Captain, or Master, or Master Gunner is dead in the voyage.

'And this ceremony of giving of guns is also in use whensoever any prime passenger, or the Captain of the ship, is to leave the ship and go to the shore.'

The fleet saluting HMS Dreadnought

There is an interesting Admiralty instruction that ships are not to fire salutes above Gravesend, and the origin of the order is that, on an occasion when Queen Elizabeth was quietly looking out of a window in the Palace at Greenwich, a ship in the river saluted; shotted rounds were used at that time for saluting purposes, and one of these came within an uncomfortable distance of the Queen, hence the order.

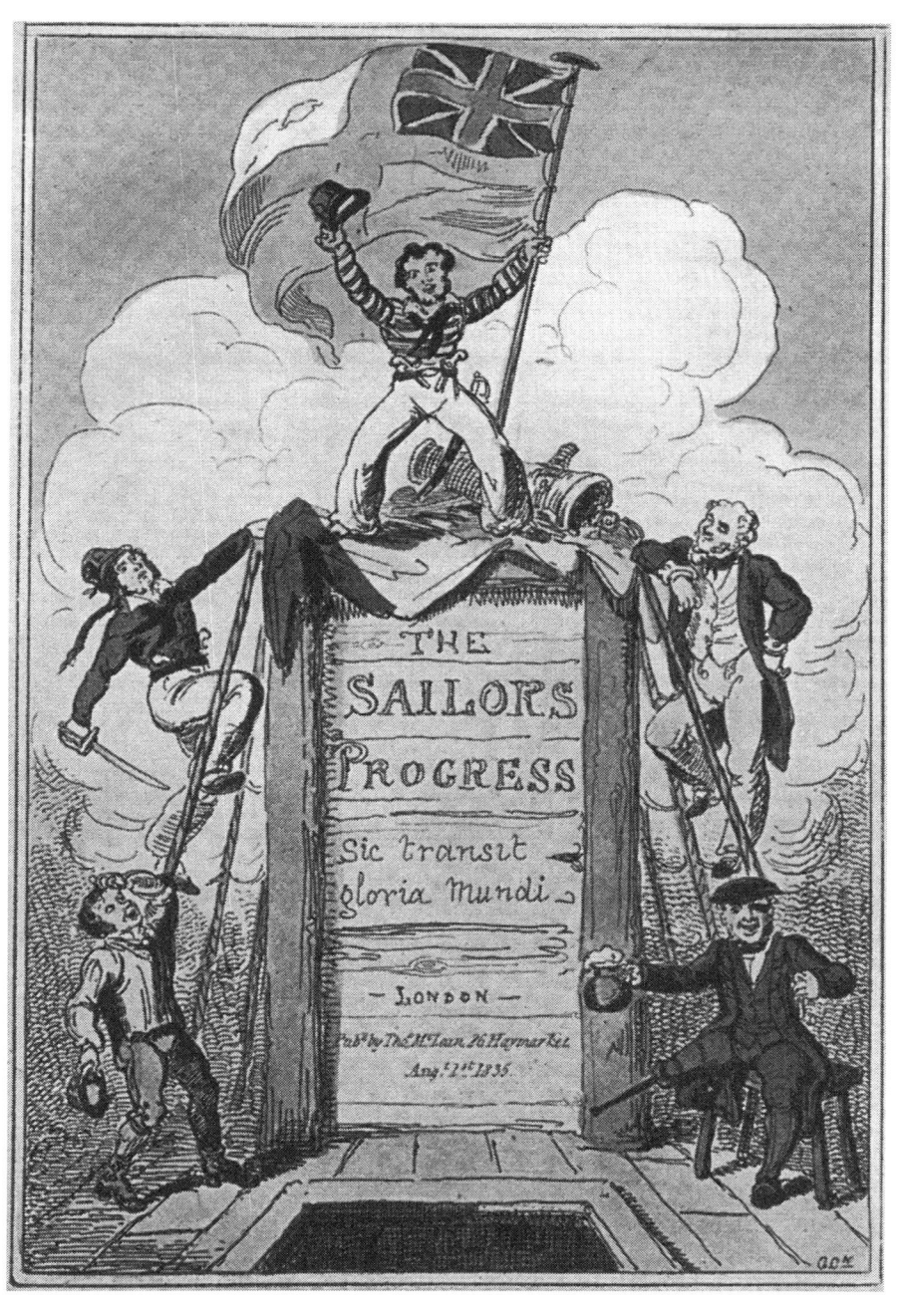

Salutes at funerals

The firing of salutes at funerals owes its origin to the old superstition that the evil spirits were scared away by noise, and the more noise made, the less chance had these spirits of being present during the ceremony.

Scandalise, to

A sail: To lower the peak, and thus to reduce the area holding the wind.

A yard: Synonymous with 'a-cockbill,' to set the yard aslant. The symbol of mourning.

Schooner

A schooner

It is related that, in 1713, Andrew Robinson, a ship-builder of Gloucester, Massachusetts, had a vessel of a new type on the stocks, and up to the date of her launch had not decided how he would describe her.

As she left the ways, a bystander cried, "Oh! look, how she scoons!" Upon which Robinson said, "A schooner let her be." And she was.

Scoff, to

To eat.

Scotchman, a

A piece of wood placed over an object to prevent ropes touching it.

Scran

Food.

To 'scoff the whole of the scran,' is to eat all there is going.

Scran bag

This was a bag in which waste bread and biscuits were collected, and no doubt used for the pigs which were formerly carried on board.

The modern use is that of a bag in which all clothing and articles left lying about, are placed. The bag is brought up on deck once or twice a week and the contents returned to the owners on payment of an inch of yellow soap.

Screw propellers

The screw propeller was introduced into the Navy in 1840. The first screw-propeller ships built were the *Archimedes* in 1838 and the *Rattler* (U.S.A.) in 1844.

Twin screws were introduced in 1863.

Archimedes

Scrimshanker

One who gets out of a job of work.

Scupper, to

To kill.

In sailing ship days anyone washed into the lee scuppers by a big sea coming onboard, stood a good chance of being killed.

Sea lawyer

One who will argue to any length.

Settle a rope with a weight on the end, to

To ease a little.

Sewed

A ship resting on the ground where the water has fallen, so as to afford no hope of floating until lightened or the return of the tide floats her, is said to be 'sewed' by as much as the difference between the surface of the water and the ship's floating mark.

If not left quite dry, she 'sews' to such a point. If the water leaves her a couple of feet, she is 'sewed' two feet.

Shackle

Derived from the Anglo-Saxon '*sceacul*,' the link of a chain.

Sheathing of ships

From the very earliest times the protection of the underwater part of a ship's timbers from the ravages of the teredo worm was a matter of urgent importance.

The Romans, as is seen in the galleys of the Emperor Caligula now visible in Lake Nemi, used lead, but the art was forgotten, and it was not till the fifteenth century that the *Santa Anna* was experimentally sheathed with lead.

About the same time it was a common practice to sheath the under-water part of a ship's timbers with soft wood as a protection. Lead was also in common use in 1660–1685, the trouble with the latter being that it was easily stripped off.

Copper was tried in 1762, but its general introduction was delayed for some years owing to the difficulty of overcoming the galvanic action set up between the copper and the iron bolts of the vessel's hull.

Eventually the trouble was met by using only copper bolts in the under-water part of the hull.

Shipmate

A term once dearer than brother, but the habit of short cruises is weakening it (from Smyth's *Sailor's Word Book*).

Shoregoing bloke

Describes men of all professions other than seafaring.

Show a leg

An exclamation from the boatswain's mate or Master-at-arms for people to show that they are awake on being called. Often 'Show a leg and turn out' (Smyth's *Sailor's Word Book*).

Another expression used is 'Rouse and Shine.'

Shrouds

In the early days when rope gear was of doubtful quality, a ship's mast was supported by innumerable stays: so numerous, in fact, that they practically obscured the mast from view in the same way as a corpse is covered by a shroud.

Sick bay

Formerly called the 'sick berth,' the latter term probably introduced by Lord St. Vincent in May 1798.

At this time ships still had the square forecastle bulkhead. Round bows to ships were introduced in 1811, and the 'sick berth' formed a bay.

Signalling, methods of

Semaphore

Invented by a Frenchman, Claude Chappe, in 1793.

In 1805 the Admiralty adopted a mechanical signalling device consisting of six shutters in a framework, designed by Lord George Murray.

Communication was maintained with Devonport through twenty-seven intermediate stations.

A time signal could be made daily by the Admiralty at 1.00 p.m., and be acknowledged in three minutes.

In 1816 Admiral Popham introduced semaphores as we know them to-day, except that they were mounted at the masthead.

Signalling by Morse, including flashing, was not introduced until late in the nineteenth century, and when first proposed met with much opposition, mainly from doubts whether ratings were capable of memorising the various symbols.

Flashing received a great impetus when electric lighting was introduced into H.M. ships.

Signalling using semaphore

Signal personnel

Signal officers were recognised as such in Nelson's time, being assisted by midshipmen, and seamen to hoist flags.

1816

The first signal ratings were introduced with the rate of second-class petty officers, and the title of Yeoman of Signals.

1860

The rate of Yeoman of Signals became a first-class rate, and a new second-class rate was introduced with the title of Signalman.

1870

The rates of Signalman second and third class, and signal boy, were introduced.

1888

Organised instruction in signalling was commenced, the first signal school being started in H.M.S. *Victory* at Portsmouth.

1895

Commander Tufnell was appointed Commanding Officer of the Signal School, and Superintendent of Signal Schools, which were by then established at the three home ports.

1903

Signal school at Portsmouth transferred to H.M.S. *Hercules*.

1905

Signal school was transferred to the Royal Naval Barracks.

1922

Signal schools at Devonport and Chatham were closed down and all training carried out at Portsmouth.

Wireless

The late Admiral of the Fleet Sir Henry Jackson carried out experiments in wireless at the same time as Signor Marconi and contributed largely to the discovery of the use of wireless waves for signalling purposes.

Wireless was first installed in one of H.M. ships for trial in 1899, largely as the result of experiments carried out by Sir Henry Jackson.

The trials led to further research and the apparatus was put under the charge of the torpedo department, volunteers from any branch being employed as personnel.

1906

The Telegraphist branch was formed.

1914

As wireless grew in importance and reliability it was decided to hand it over to the Signal branch, though research work continued to be carried out in H.M.S. *Vernon*.

1918

The experimental department of W/T was transferred to the Signal School.

Signal books

Various attempts to communicate between ships at sea by means of flags were made from about the ninth century, and a secret book entitled *Fighting Instructions,* containing such simple flag signals as were considered necessary, was issued by the Admiralty in 1647.

It was left to private individuals to arrange further signals for the conduct of the Fleet, and these were issued at the expense of the officer commanding the Fleet.

Up to 1647 it was the custom for ships of war to gather round the senior officer's ship each evening to receive orders. In this year, however, the Admiralty issued a more elaborate plan, entitled *Instructions for Sailing*. In 1653 a 'weft' of the ensign and jack, also the red, white and blue flags, were made use of: the latter were also flags of command. In 1672–1673 the signals were added to and printed as *Fighting Instructions,* and these formed the basis of the instructions for the next hundred years. In 1689 the first manuscript signal book proper was produced. Up to this time the signals were entirely embodied in the *Fighting Instructions*.

In 1691 the *Fighting Instructions* of 1673 were revised and issued by Admiral Russell, four more single flags being added. Although Admiral Russell was given the credit for the work, it is more than probable that it was written by Admiral Torrington. They were again revised in 1703 by Admiral Rooke, and issued as the *Permanent Fighting Instructions*. This signal book contained a series of well-engraved plates of ships flying the various signals contained in the *Fighting Instructions,* each properly coloured and with its signification below. It was intended for the use of junior officers who did not have access to the secret instructions. This method of tallying the signals, although quite new to the British Navy, appears to have been in use in the French Navy quite twenty years before.

Admiral Russell

In 1746, John Millan published another signal book, which contained sixteen flags with their significations and the articles and pages of the *Fighting Instructions* to which the signal referred. In addition the book contained a Table of Salutes, Night Signals, etc., and the Flags of all Nations. The book concluded with a summary of the Articles of War, and various items of information, one among others being that if the Commander swears or curses he is fined one shilling, a warrant officer one penny, and men to wear a wooden collar, and others are that drunk officers were fined two days' pay, and men placed in irons until sober. The Commander could award up to twelve strokes with the cat on the bare back.

The next book of 1756 is another manuscript book, now in the Royal United Services Institution.

In 1762 another manuscript signal book was produced entitled *General printed and additional Signals delivered out by Sir Edward Hawke*. This book illustrates twenty-six flags, and two more pendants were added but not illustrated.

Up to this time signals had made but little headway, the flags merely indicating single meanings according to where they were hoisted. From now onwards, however, they really began to make headway, and a signal book of Lord Rodney, which he used in his fight against De Grasse in 1782, shows twenty-three new flags.

To sum up the era of single flag signalling: in 1746 there were sixteen flags to express 144 signals, and in 1780 there were fifty flags, each hoisted on an average in seven different positions and expressing in all 330 signals.

Twenty-five years later (1805) the Trafalgar signal book contained 400 signals, not including Popham's Code.

Single-flag signals were all very well, provided the signals were few, but as the number increased the system broke down, and in 1778 Admirals Kempenfelt, Home and Knowles set to work independently to produce a method of signalling which would be suitable to the requirements of the Navy.

The methods introduced were:

1. The Numerary Method, which was actually invented by a Frenchman, Le Bourdonnais, about 1738. It was to allot one flag for each number from 0 to 9, and by combining the flags so to obtain any desired number.
2. The Tabular Method invented by Admiral Knowles.

A chequered table similar to a chess-board is ruled out, and an arrangement of flags and numbers noted thereon as in the diagram below:

	Red	White	Blue
Red	1	4	7
White	2	5	8
Blue	3	6	9

The signal corresponding to 4 will then be a white flag over a red one. This method was chosen by Lord Howe, probably because with a sixteen-sided square he could make 256 signals as opposed to 99 by the numerary method.

The Alphabetical Method was not introduced till 1812, when Popham issued his revised code.

In 1790 a purser of the Navy, by name John McArthur, produced a code which was undoubtedly better than that of Howe, but as it is nicely put: 'Some scruples of delicacy intervened in the adoption of any new plan of signals which would supersede that of Earl Howe's Numerary Code,' and it was not adopted. Lord Hood, however, was impressed with it, and made McArthur his secretary.

These books were apparently quite simple, but in one case proved too much for a certain Captain of a line of battleship, who, being unable to understand the signal, threw the book on the deck and exclaimed in broad Scots, "Damn me, up with the helm and gang into the middle of it."

With the system enumerated above, whereby various Admirals produced their own codes, the inevitable result was that signals on one station were unintelligible on another. This state of affairs was ended by Lord Howe's second book in 1790, called the *Signal book for ships of war,* and henceforth signals were universal on all stations. In this book the tabular or chess-board method was abolished.

The first vocabulary signal book was produced by Sir Home Popham, who obtained his ideas for the book from a treatise on Seamanship of 1796, written by Gower of the East India Company. In 1816 this book was revised by Popham and issued to the Fleet as an official *Vocabulary Signal Book,* remained in force eleven years, was again revised and issued in three volumes: (1) *General Signal Book,* containing evolutionary and battle signals denoted by numeral flags, (2) *Vocabulary Signal Book,* containing words and sentences and denoted by alphabetical flags,

(3) *Night and Fog Signals*. Revisions of the books took place at intervals *in* succeeding years.

In 1889 the *Fleet Manual* was issued, also an auxiliary signal book. The *Fleet Signal Book* came into use in 1898, and superseded the *General Signal Book* and *Fleet Manual,* and at the same time the *Flotilla Signal Book* superseded the *Auxiliary Signal Book.*

These were used with slight variations until the issue of the *Signal Manual* of 1917, together with the *General Signal Book.*

Fleet Codes, volumes I and II, were introduced in 1918, and superseded the *General Signal Book* and *Vocabulary Signal Book.*

Various other books have been produced at odd times, notably the *Wireless Signal Instructions* in 1914.

As regards signals for merchant ships, no code existed till 1804, and here again Sir Home Popham produced a book of *Commercial and Military Signals* for the use of the ships of the East India Company. In 1817 Captain Marryat drew up the forerunner of the modern *Commercial Code,* the book being in six parts: Names of Men-of-War, Names of Merchantmen, Ports, etc., Sentences, and Two Volumes of Vocabulary.

In 1848, owing to the enormous increase in the number of ships, a more ample code was found necessary, and a Committee appointed by the Board of Trade considered the matter. They found that the numeral system should be abandoned, and in lieu chose 18 flags, which by using two, three or four flags in a hoist allowed of nearly 79,000 combinations. The flags omitted were X, Y, Z and the vowels, the Committee wording their reasons as follows: 'To avoid the use of objectionable words in our own, and foreign languages.' The flags adopted were those in use in the *Fleet Code* to-day, with the exception of F and L, which were altered later. This book was issued in 1857 under the name of *The Commercial Code of Signal* for use by all nations, the name being changed to *International Code* in 1880. In 1887 the code was again revised; the result proving unsatisfactory, a complete recasting of the code was undertaken, and brought into force for all nations in 1901. The letters previously objected to were introduced. The colours of the F and L flags were slightly altered, and the code produced in its present form.

This completes the brief outline of the story of signals for use by ships at sea. As regards the actual hoisting or showing of the flags, the earliest method was for the flag to be nailed to a staff and carried about. Later it became customary to sew the hoist to a sleeve of canvas which was slipped over the staff, large flags being sewn to a strip of canvas and tied to the staff. Finally the flag was sewn to a piece of rope which could be made fast to haulyards, but as these were only led into the top and not to the upper deck a seaman had to go aloft every time a signal was made. These methods were, of course, insufferably slow, and probably impeded the development of signals. Signal haulyards were not, in any case, brought down to the upper deck till after 1672, for the Duke of Marlborough's journal of that date speaks of a seaman set at the foretopmast head with the 'Flag of Defiance' loose in his arms ready to hoist.

Silence in a man-of-war

Nothing is more detrimental to the carrying out of work than noise. When Napoleon surrendered himself on board H.M.S. *Bellerophon* in July 1815 (shortly after Waterloo), he remarked as the ship was getting under way to carry him to Torbay, "Your method of performing this evolution is quite different to the French. What I admire most in your ship is the extreme silence and orderly conduct of your men. On board a French ship everyone calls and gives orders and they gabble like so many geese."

Previous to his quitting the *Bellerophon* he said, "There has been less noise in this ship, where there are 600 men, during the whole time I have been in her than there was on board the *Spervier* [a French frigate], with only 100 men, in the passage from Isle d'Aix to Baspue Roads."

Skipper

This is a corruption of the Scandinavian word for ship, namely '*schiffe*.'

Slops

Derived from 'slip,' meaning any garment easily adjusted.

A famous cloth merchant of the time of King Henry VIII (1509–1547) is described as appearing before that monarch in a plain russet coat, and a pair of white kersey 'slops,' the stockings of the same piece being sewn to his slops.

Snob

A ship's cobbler.

Snotty (midshipman)

This appears to have been a term of abuse, for in 1795 Mr. Locke, boatswain of the *Rattlesnake*, was ordered by Mr. Coffin, the Second Lieutenant, to stop beating a midshipman. Mr. Locke replied that 'he was only beating a snotty midshipman.'

Snub a cable, to

To check it.

South wind (or north wind) in anything, a

Nothing in it.

Speaking-trumpet

One is said to have been used by Alexander in 335 B.C. It was brought into notice by Morland in 1670.

Spell. To give a spell.

From *Boteler's Dialogues* (1685):

'To do a spell is to do any work or labour for a short time, and then to leave it successively to some other fresh men to take their turns at it; and so it is called a "fresh spell" when fresh men come to work, as when one company pumps one hundred strokes in a glass (that is in the space of an hour) it is termed their spell.

'Likewise in rowing in the boat, when one says to another: "Give a spell," it is as much as to say, "Row in

Spinnaker

A spinnaker sail

This sail was first set in the cutter *Niobe* in 1865, and the sail was for the first few months called a 'niob.'

The *Niobe*, however, had a more famous rival the *Sphinx*, and she almost simultaneously set a similar sail. The sailors called her the *Spinx*, and they called the peculiar sail the 'spinxer,' which name prevailed over the word 'niob,' and became the common word 'spinnaker.'

Spliced

Married.

Splicing the main brace

The expression sprang from the custom of giving a man a tot of rum as a reward when he had been employed on the difficult and highly skilled task of putting a splice in the main brace.

Split yarn, to have everything on a

Everything ready at a moment's notice.

Square yards with another, to

To settle or to have it out with another person.

Squeegee band

A band of music composed of volunteers from the ship's company.

Starboard

The word is a survival of the days when ships were steered by an oar on the quarter, called a 'steerboard.'

This oar was always placed on the same side, which in time became known as the 'steerboard' or 'starboard' side.

Station, to keep

Derived from a ship keeping her station in the fleet.

Used in conversation to order a man to keep his appointed place, as for instance when marching.

Stay, a long

Used in cable work to explain that a lot of cable is out and bearing well ahead.

Formerly used when the cable and the main stay were in line.

Stay, a short

Used in cable work to explain that little cable is out.

Formerly used when the cable and the fore stay were in line.

Stretch off the land, a

When a ship was beating, say, for instance, up-channel, it was only natural that when approaching shore everyone was on the top line for going about. This accomplished, there was then nothing immediate to do and a chance came for a rest or sleep.

Sub-lieutenant

This rank was introduced into the Royal Navy by Lord St. Vincent, but did not, however, take root in the Service, and soon died out, not to be revived till half a century later.

Sun over the fore yard

Time for the first drink.

Sunset

It was laid down that the sentry should fire his rifle at sunset. The reason for this was a relic of the days of the flintlock rifle, when it was done in order to ensure that the rifle was freshly loaded and primed for the hours of darkness.

Surge

From *Boteler's Dialogues* (1685):
'And this word Surge is also used when, heaving at the Capstan, the cable chances to slip back again, for then we use to say that the cable surges.'

Swabtail

A mean fellow.

Sway the main, to

To exaggerate.

Swifter

The bars of a capstan are 'swifted' by passing a 'rope swifter' over all the ends, and bousing it well taut.

Tabling

A broad hem on the edge of a ship's sails to strengthen them in the part which is sewn to the bolt-rope.

Tankie

Slang term for the midshipman attached to the Navigating Officer.
Also used for the Captain of the hold.

Tar (as a sailor's name)

The name is derived from the ancient habit of a sailor of tarring his trousers, in order to make them waterproof; hence also the term 'tarry breeks.'

Tattoo

Derived from the old Dutch '*taptoe*,' meaning the time to close the taps or taverns.
At a certain hour the drummers marched from post to post in the town beating their drums; 'first post' would be the signal of their having taken their place to commence their rounds, whilst 'last post' would be sounded when they reached the end of the round.

Till all's blue

Carried to the utmost.
A phrase derived from the idea of a vessel making out of port, and getting into blue water.

Time

From as early as the eighteenth century the hours in a ship were given by sounding the watch bell, the time being reckoned by a 'half-hour sand glass.'
The four hours naturally gave the eight bells of the eight half-hours they contained.

Toe pitch, to

To be accused of an offence against discipline.

Toe the line

Derived from the custom of lining up along the seam of the deck.

Toe the pitch

Derived similarly to 'toe the line,' but in this case the pitch of the seam is referred to.

Togs

A very old slang term for clothes.

Tom Pepper

He was supposed to have been kicked out of hell for lying, and hence the use of the term to describe a liar.

Tonnage

The Bordeaux wine trade was the earliest, and for two centuries one of the most important, branches of English maritime traffic; ships were therefore measured by their carrying capacity in Bordeaux casks. The first arithmetical rule for calculating a ship's tonnage was devised in 1582, and that rule made the net, or cask, tonnage nearly the same as the average cargo.

The unit of measurement was therefore the tun of wine in two butts of 252 gallons, which in 1626 were estimated to occupy 60 cubic feet of space.

After 1628 the method of reckoning was by taking the length of keel, greatest breadth of beam, and depth, multiplying these and dividing by one hundred.

Top one's boom, to

To start off, to leave.

Top-gallant

The old derivation from 'top garland' is now discredited. The word is met with in 1514. 'Top' is the noun and 'gallant' distinguishes the top-gallant from the lower tops as making a brave or gallant show in comparison.

Topmast, topsails

With the advent of the fighting ship there appeared the 'top,' which was placed right at the top of the mast as a position from which stones, javelins, etc., could be thrown at the enemy.

There a flagpole was erected, and later the idea of hoisting a sail on this pole was adopted; hence both the sail hoisted thereon and the pole or mast received the designation 'top.'

Tot or tott (of rum)

A drinking-cup somewhat smaller than the regulation half-pint, by which a surplus is left in the distribution of the regular allowance of grog, and is awarded to the cook of each mess for the day for his trouble (Smyth's *Sailor's Word Book*).

Treenails

Long cylindrical oak or other hard wood pins driven through the planks and timbers of a ship to connect the various parts.

Trick, a

A turn, e.g. a trick at the wheel.

Trinity House

This may be termed the Cradle of the Navy, for it is the oldest Guild of Mariners in England, and at one time had the charge of the Naval Storehouse of the Crown at Deptford, and the conduct of, 'The Navy Royall.'

The headquarters at Trinity House, Tower Hill, were completed in 1798.

The old title was 'The Guild, Fraternity, or Brotherhood of the Most Glorious and Undivided Trinity, and of St. Clements in the Parish Church of Deptford Strond' (or foreshore).

There is no doubt that, long before the formation of a Corporation of Trinity House, there existed a rich fraternity of seamen and pilots at Deptford.

The first charter was granted by Henry VIII in 1514, was suspended at the Commonwealth, and restored at the Restoration, and the Charter of James II is the one under which the Corporation acts at present.

Up to the end of the Stuart period there was little to distinguish men-of-war from merchant vessels, and Trinity House not only designed ships, but were also responsible for their fitting out in every respect.

When, however, the men-of-war became a distinct class from the merchant vessel, the naval control of the Corporation ceased. The touch with the Navy, however, is still maintained, especially with the Hydrographical Department.

From the start the Corporation was responsible for the provision of qualified pilots, and the care and maintenance of sea marks. The first lighthouse appears to have been erected at Caister in 1600 followed soon after by two at Lowestoft. Early harbour lights were coal lights in open braziers, and later candle-lights. Illumination of lighthouses has passed through the stages of coal and wood fires, candles and oil-lamps, to the modern methods of the petroleum vapour burner and electric lamps.

It was during the religious troubles of Edward VI's reign that the Corporation changed its name to the 'Corporation of Trinity House' to avoid the confiscation of their property.

A grant of arms was made in 1573, and their flag, granted in Tudor times, is a red ensign with four galleons in the fly. During the mutiny at the Nore in 1797 Trinity

Trinity House

House assisted in the removal of navigational marks, and in 1803, on the threat of French invasion, maintained and manned ten frigates in the Thames, moored across The Hope, for the defence of London.

In 1836 Trinity House was given complete control of all lighthouses and navigational marks.

Up to 1853 light dues were paid by ships to Trinity House, but in this year the dues were transferred to the Board of Trade, and the Corporation receives annually a sum of money to cover the expenses to be incurred.

Up to 1874 they examined the officers of the Navigation Branch of the Royal Navy.

Trinity House consists of a Master, now H.R.H. the Duke of Connaught, a Deputy Master, Vice-Admiral Mansell, and nine Elder Brethren, and about two hundred Younger Brethren.

The Elder Brethren still control the various charities, and maintain sixty-five almshouses at Mile End.

Trinity House furnishes the expert advisers to the Port of London Authority, the Southampton and Harwich Harbour Boards. Assessors drawn from the Elder Brethren are known as Trinity Masters, and also assist the President and Judges in the Admiralty Courts in marine cases.

By ancient privilege the Elder Brethren act as Royal Pilots to His Majesty, when afloat in pilotage waters, on state occasions.

Other duties of the Corporation are the destruction and removal of wrecks, and they are responsible for the lighthouses, beacons, and buoys, etc., for some 2,400 miles of the Coast of England, Wales and Channel Isles.

In Scotland similar duties are carried out by the Northern Lighthouse Board, and in Ireland by the Irish Lighthouse Board.

Repairing a Trinity House buoy

Tyminoguy

From Blanckney's *Naval Expositor*:

'A rope, one end nailed to the outside of the stock of an anchor stowed at the bows, and the other fastened or belayed to the ship's sides on the forecastle.

'Its use for preventing the fore sheets (when getting under sail) dropping down between the anchor stock and the ship's side.'

Present-day use of this term is to describe an ingenious device or 'gadget.'

Ullage

When anything is taken from a cask, what is left is the 'ullage.' The word is used to describe incompetence. A 'regular ullage' is a useless fellow. Another expression is 'a proper ullage.'

Uniform, naval

The first definite information that we have of clothing worn by seamen comes down to us from the Roman invasion, when we learn that the Veneti put to sea from the Loire in speedy longboats, and that the sails and clothing of the crew were dyed a light blue colour, presumably to lessen the chance of being seen.

Later, with the arrival of the Danes, black seems to have been the predominant colour.

Just before the Norman invasion clothing of a blue colour was worn, and, as a defensive costume, leather jerkins were introduced.

Middle ages Seamen wore the ordinary clothing of the common people, with the addition of a jerkin with the Royal, or feudal lord's cognizance, emblazoned on it.

1385
The armed forces of the Crown wore the sign of St. George before and behind.

A sea-gown of coarse frieze, girdled at the waist, and falling to the knees was worn, with a fur cap.

Tudor times The colours changed to green and white.

Reign of Queen Mary Sky-blue colour was reverted to, as we learn that the seamen of Sir Hugh Willoughby's expedition were dressed in that colour.

Early Stuart Colours and facings were changed to red and yellow, and so remained, till the establishment of the naval officers' uniform in 1748, with the exception of the Commonwealth period, when the colours were buff and brown.

During the whole of the above periods, persons who fancied other colours for wear on board wore exactly what they liked, and one reads of red coats faced with blue, scarlet and silver, etc.

1623
Slop clothing on repayment was first issued by the Crown in order to avoid 'nastie beastliness by disease and unwholesome ill smells in the ship,' and this issue must have led to a certain uniformity in the seamen's clothing.

Fancy names for clothing

A Portsmouth slop seller's sign, 1790:

>   MORGAN, Mercer and Sea Draper,
>   No. 85, opposite the Fountain Inn,
>   High Street

'Sailors rigged complete from stem to stern, viz. chapeau, napeau, flying jib and flesh bag, inner pea, outer pea, and cold defender; rudder case and service to the same; up haulers and down traders, fore shoes, lacings, gaskets, etc.'

> 'With Canvas bags
> To hold your cags
> And chests to sit upon;
> Clasp knives your meat
> To cut and eat
> When ship does lay along.'

1655
The slop lists included canvas jackets and drawers, cotton drawers and waistcoats, shirts, cotton stockings, shoes, thrummed caps.

The only colours mentioned in connection with the seaman's clothing are buff and blue.

1663
Red was introduced, and amongst the slops issued we read: red caps, Monmouth caps, yarn stockings, Irish stockings, blue and white shirts, cotton waistcoats and drawers, neat's leather shoes, blue neckcloths, canvas suits and 'rugs.' Jackets and trousers are not mentioned, and presumably they were covered by 'canvas suits.'

1689–1727
Officers wore the civilian dress of the period.

Common Sailor

1719–1750
Seamen wore grey jackets, striped waistcoats, and red 'wide kneed' trousers supplied by slop sellers, also kerchiefs of various colours round the neck, flat topped, three-cornered hats or leather caps faced with red, and not infrequently a 'petticoat' (or short coat) of canvas or baize.

We now come to the introduction of a uniform dress for naval officers.

With the issue of Order in Council of February 10th, 1748, defining relative rank between naval and military officers, and also amongst sea-officers themselves, an attempt was made to distinguish the different ranks by their dress. The Admiralty orders are dated April 13th, 1748, and direct the uniform clothing to be worn 'at all proper times.' Patterns for flag-officers' uniform were lodged at the Admiralty; for other combatant officers (including midshipmen) at the Navy Office and at Plymouth dockyard. Only combatant ranks were ordered to wear the uniform clothing.

The adoption of such a uniform had been urged on the First Lord of the Admiralty (the Duke of Bedford) by a delegation from the Navy Club (a dining club and benevolent society, whose latter functions still exist in the Royal Naval Benevolent Society) in 1746. In its details this naval uniform of 1748 corresponded with that of the relative rank in the Army. The colour selected for the coat was blue, with white cuffs and with gold facings for the full dress of flag-officers, and with gold facings on white lapels for the undress. The selection of white as the subsidiary colour (instead of red, which Service opinion favoured as being the 'military' colour) has been attributed to King George II, who illustrated his taste for blue and white as harmonious colours by citing the Duchess of Bedford's riding habit of these colours. This story first appeared more than eighty years later, being told as a reminiscence of Admiral of the Fleet the Hon. John Forbes. Its appearance in print resulted in the decision to alter the white facings to red in 1832; but the lack of harmony in the colours proved the justness of George II's taste, and the original white was reverted to.

In 1787 uniform regulations were first issued for 'warrant' officers (which then included masters, surgeons and pursers). In 1805 surgeons were first given a distinguishing uniform; and in 1807 masters and pursers.

1805

Seamen wore what they liked, but for all that uniformity of dress obtained amongst them. In bad weather the seaman wore a 'wrap rascal' coat or 'rug' of frieze and a leather, felt, or tarred canvas apron reaching below the knees, woollen stockings and knee breeches.

For work on board he wore blue or white trousers, blue, green, or red serge frock (duck or flannel).

On his head a straw hat, a fur cap, or a woollen tam-o'-shanter. Some Captains insisted that their men should wear frocks or shirts of the same colour.

Ashore a smart seaman wore a short blue jacket with a row of flat gold or brass buttons down the right side, and on the cuffs. Trousers were either of blue cloth or of white duck, cut extremely loose and a shade too long so that they nearly covered the feet.

White stockings, shoes like dancing-pumps with silver buckles. Plain red, blue, or white shirts with an open collar, or a jersey with blue and white horizontal stripes were worn. Round the throat, loosely knotted, was a silk handkerchief. A scarlet or canary yellow waistcoat was popular. The jacket and waistcoat were frequently decorated with ribbons sewn down the seams.

A low-crowned, black tarpaulin hat with a ribbon painted with the name of the ship, or a motto, formed the usual headgear. Officers and men were clean-shaven, but pigtails were popular from 1800 to 1815.

The latter were worn doubled up on week days, but on smart occasions they were allowed to hang down, reaching, in some cases, as far as the waist. If the hair did not suffice, teased out oakum was plaited in.

Earrings were also worn from the belief that their use improved the eyesight.

It was not till 1857 that a uniform dress was ordered for the men. Changes in uniform were made in succeeding years as regards details, the principal ones being as described below.

Hats

Nelson in 1781

Hats are not mentioned in the regulations until 1825. Three-cornered hats, however, with a silk cockade of George I, first appear to have been worn, changed at the end of the century to two flaps and worn athwartships one bent down in front, the other standing straight up behind. Later both flaps stood up, with tassels dangling over each shoulder. In 1825 a cocked hat to be worn fore and aft with full and undress was ordered. At sea a round black hat, bound with silk, narrow silk band and black buckle, black cockade and loop, finished off with a strip of gold lace and button, known as the lightning conductor, or a cap of blue cloth with gold band and a crown, was added in 1847.

Coat collars

From 1748 to 1774.—There were none.
From 1774 to 1787.—Flat collar.
1787 onwards.—Stand up.

In 1825 full-dress collars were used to carry the badges of profession. Masters wore the three-anchor badge of the Navy Office; physicians, snake and anchor; pursers, the two anchors crossed.

In 1827 all collars were made to stand up, and the colour was changed from blue to white.

Cuffs

The first kind were made full in order to allow for the lace on the waistcoat sleeves to protrude and fall over the hands. When the first full dress was abolished, 1767, smaller cuffs came in, all ranks down to Lieutenant wearing a slash of blue. In 1768 Lieutenants' cuffs and lapels changed to white. In 1774 blue was adopted by all ranks in undress, white being retained for full dress. In 1787 they were laced with gold, three for Admirals and two for Senior Captains, one for Junior ditto and Commanders, the latter having blue facings.

At this period a Lieutenant's undress coat was distinguished by a white piping. Warrant officers, i.e. masters, surgeons, pursers, gunners, boatswains and carpenters, were given uniform and blue round caps, but no full dress. In 1795 white cuffs disappeared for all ranks, but reappeared in 1812, and finally disappeared in 1827, when they were replaced by white slashes as now. The distinction rings were removed. The spacing of buttons was also used to distinguish rank. In 1774 Senior Captains had 12 by threes, Junior ditto 12 by twos, and Commanders 12 regular. In 1783 flag officer rank was noted by their buttonholes, Admirals equidistant, Vice in threes, Rear in twos in undress, whilst in full dress they had three, two, or one row of embroidery on the cuffs, similar to Generals.

Buttons

The earliest button was of bright metal, flat, having a rose; another type was round and smooth. In 1774 an engraved anchor and cable on flat buttons was substituted. In 1787

Costume of the Royal Navy, 1847.
Captain, Flag Officer and Commander (undress)

the cable was removed and an anchor surrounded by laurel was substituted, an anchor in an oval being worn by officers under flag rank. Warrant officers same as Captain 1774 pattern.

The crown was revived in 1812, but embossed, not engraved.

In 1827 special buttons were ordered to distinguish different branches—gunners, bo'suns, and carpenters wearing only an anchor. The engineers' first device was a beam engine surmounted by a crown.

In 1843 military branch officers had the buttons regularly spaced on double-breasted coats. Civilian branch, single-breasted with buttons spaced by twos, threes or fours according to their profession. In 1856 all buttons were made the same and as at present.

Waistcoats

Waistcoats were originally white kerseymere altered to white cloth in 1774, the former material being reverted to in 1825. Up to 1774 they were laced for Flag Officers, Captains and Commanders, but Flag Officers only continued to wear laced waistcoats up to 1787.

Breeches

Prior to 1805 breeches were worn, but in this year pantaloons were adopted by officers who had taken to the Hessian boot. In 1825 kerseymere knee breeches and white and blue pantaloons were allowed. Later, in 1827, breeches were only to be worn at drawing-rooms.

Footgear had been generally shoes, which were gradually supplanted by the half boot introduced in 1825.

Epaulettes

These came in 1795, as a result, it is said, of representations made by officers who went abroad: military officers, owing to their epaulettes, were accorded marks of respect, etc., which were not accorded to their naval brothers who lacked them. They were called swabs, owing to their limp nature. Admirals wore two with one, two or three stars, according to rank. Captains over three years had two plain epaulettes. Under three years one on right shoulder. Commanders one on left shoulder. This arrangement remained till 1812 when all Captains and Commanders were given two epaulettes with a silver crown and anchor for Senior Captains, anchor for Junior, and nothing for Commanders, and Lieutenants were given one plain, to be worn on the right shoulder.

Swords

Swords were first made uniform in 1805, and ten years later masters of the fleet and all non-executive officers were ordered to have black hand-grips, and the blades were not blued. In 1843 the white grip was brought in for all officers except warrant officers (gunner, carpenter, etc.).

The following is a description of the uniform worn by naval officers of the *Viceroy of Ireland* yacht in 1823:

A modern sword

Garter blue coat, embroidered on chest, cuffs and collar with sprigs of shamrock; white breeches with gold garters, hat and feathers, and sword. Undress: plain brown coat with shamrock buttons, buff breeches and waistcoat.

I will now just enumerate the main changes that took place after 1825.

1827

First mention of petty officers' badges, which were white. Coats first made with skirts, and gold-laced trousers introduced; also round hats for warrant officers and midshipmen.

1828

Full-dress coats were ordered to be buttoned up.

1830

The facings were changed from white to scarlet. Gold-laced trousers were abolished and white breeches ceased to become a part of the naval officer's uniform. Later in the year gold-laced trousers were reintroduced for flag officers only.

1831

White and blue trousers were regulated for full dress, according to season, and gold-laced trousers reintroduced for all military officers.

1832

Master of the fleet dressed as Commanders. Civil officers were given the same uniform as commissioned officers, but single-breasted. The buttons were three and three for physicians and surgeons. Secretaries two and two. Undress sword belt was introduced. Some misunderstanding having occurred warrant officers were forbidden to wear cocked hats.

1833

Caps introduced with gold lace band.

1843

White facings reintroduced for collars and slash. Blue cuffs. Stripes for flag officers only.

1846

Two epaulettes for Lieutenants, one for Mates.

1847

Frock coat established, and scales for wear on board abolished.

1856

The curl was introduced for military officers, civil officers being given the same corresponding stripes without the curl and gold-laced trousers. Captains had three rows, Commanders two, Lieutenants one. The cap was given a black band, and plain gold peaks were introduced for executive officers above Lieutenants. The shape was something like the French *képi*. Dirks made uniform for midshipmen instead of swords.

1857

Uniform was introduced for men, consisting of: Blue cloth jacket, blue cloth trousers, duck frock, duck trousers, serge frock, pea jacket, black and white hats, badges.

1860

Warrant officers were given the same buttons as remainder. The peaks of executive officers' caps were oak leaved, and civil branches were given plain. Petty officer badges white and blue.

1861

Sub-lieutenants emerged from Mates, and were given one stripe. Lieutenants two, Commanders three, Captains four, Commodores a broad stripe.

1864

A.D.C. wore a sash, and civil officers coloured stripes between the gold ones. Gunnery instructors' badges, red and blue, were brought in.

1865

White trousers were abolished in full dress.

1869

Beards and hat ribbons introduced for sailors.

1877

Additional half-ring for Lieutenant of eight years' seniority.

1879

The ship jacket later called monkey-jacket introduced. Gold badges for men. Aiguillettes in lieu of sash for A.D.C.'s.

1891

Ball dress, mess dress and undress regularised. In 1891 a much needed addition was made, officers' white uniforms being introduced. Blue coats had been the only rig on hot stations. This led to the coats being made so thin that it is said an order had to be issued ordering that they should be thick enough to prevent the braces being seen through them.

1915

Engineer officers given the curl.

1918

All officers given the curl, and full dress made optional.

(Reproduced by courtesy of the Council of the Royal United Service Institution, from their *Journal* of September 1921, and of Commander R. N. Suter, Royal Navy, from his lecture on 'Naval Costume Past and Present.')

Urk, an

Slang term for a shirker.

Vernon torpedo establishment

The first torpedo was evolved in 1864 by Captain Luppis, an Austrian naval officer. It was driven by clockwork, and directed from the shore by guiding lines attached to the rudder. Captain Luppis entered into an agreement with Mr. Robert Whitehead (manager of an engine factory at Fiume) to improve and perfect the idea; and two years later the first fish torpedo was constructed.

In August 1869 a committee of gunnery officers from the Mediterranean fleet visited Fiume and reported on the invention, which had rapidly been improved under the auspices of the Austrian Government.

Their report resulted in the Admiralty appointing a committee consisting of Captain William Arthur, Captain Morgan Singer and Lieutenant Arthur Wilson (of H.M.S. *Excellent*) to carry out investigations of the possibilities of the invention, which had been kept highly secret. Mr. Whitehead was invited to England, and found himself detained in Paris on his journey by the outbreak of the Franco-Prussian War, being only released by the intervention of the British Ambassador.

Experiments were carried out in the Medway, the firing taking place from the *Oberon* against a hulk, the *Aigle*, which was sunk by the first shot.

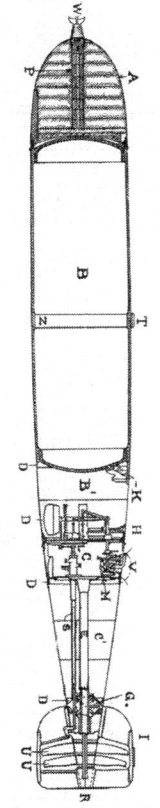

Whitehead's torpedo

The Committee recommended the purchase of the secret and rights of manufacture of the invention, for which £15,000 was paid. Manufacture was undertaken at the Royal Laboratory, Woolwich Arsenal.

The first official step taken in the Navy to study and develop torpedo work had already been taken in 1867, when Lieutenant H. C. Kane, of the *Excellent,* was directed to compile a manual on the subject, after a course of instruction at the Royal Engineering School of Submarine Mining. This manual was subsequently enlarged by Commander Fisher, and formed the basis of the instruction given. The school thus begun as a branch of the *Excellent,* was carried on in the *Vernon* (which in February 1874 was attached to the *Excellent* as tender, for Torpedo Instruction School). The growing importance and the complexity of the subject required a greater freedom and a more concentrated attention than such a subordinate position allowed; and on April 26th, 1876, the *Vernon* was separated from the *Excellent* and commissioned as a separate establishment, under Captain W. Arthur, with Commander Arthur Wilson as commander. Some account of the work of the pioneers in torpedo work in the *Vernon,* will be found in the biography of Admiral of the Fleet Sir Arthur Knyvet Wilson, by Admiral Sir Edward Bradford.

It is of interest to note that H.M.S. *Vernon* was the first of a famous type of frigate designed by Captain Sir William Symonds. She was named *Vernon* after Admiral Vernon, the Porto Bello hero of the last century, and as a compliment to Lord Vernon, a great friend and supporter of Captain Symonds'.

The figurehead, which now stands in the grounds of the Torpedo Establishment, is a very indifferent likeness of the great Admiral, both in features and in dress.

In 1886 the *Vernon* was replaced by the *Donegal,* which was renamed *Vernon*; the old *Vernon* was renamed *Actaeon,* and remained attached to the establishment.

The establishment was gradually increased, the *Vernon* (late *Donegal*) being called *Vernon I.* In 1902 *Vernon II* was added (being the *Marlborough,* launched in 1885); and in 1904 *Vernon III* (being the *Warrior,* launched in 1860).

In 1905 the Torpedo School at Sheerness was created by the hulk *Ariadne* being moored there and renamed *Actaeon*. The *Vernon's Actaeon* was transferred to Sheerness in 1916, and added to the establishment there.

(Reproduced by courtesy of the Commanding Officer, H.M.S. *Vernon*, and of Lieutenant G. B. Sayer, Royal Navy, the author of *The History of H.M.S.* Vernon, *Torpedo Establishment*.)

The Gunwharf was commenced in 1662, the contractor bearing the historic name of William Shakespeare; his workmen were paid at the establishment in Bishop Street that henceforth bore the name of 'The Shakespeare's Head.' In 1719 the officers' houses were erected; and in 1797 the armoury. Rebuilding took place in 1807.

A new Gunwharf for the Navy was commenced in 1797, and finished in 1814. The foundation-stone of the store-houses was laid by Admiral of the Fleet the Duke of Clarence (afterwards William IV) on November 28th, 1811.

The ordnance departments were reorganised in 1891, and considerable additions made to the naval administrative duties, necessitating increased accommodation. During the Great War the Admiralty took over from the War Office part of the Gunwharf for the mining school; and in October 1920 secured practically the whole of the property. The new establishment for the *Vernon* was thereupon erected at the cost of over £850,000 (including £200,000 for machinery). The end of the old establishment came on the last day of 1923, when the hulks were paid off. On January 1st, 1924, the trawler *Strathcoe* (one of the tenders attached to the establishment) was commissioned as *Vernon*, from which date the present establishment commences. The old *Vernon II*, after being sold to shipbreakers, foundered on her way up-Channel on November 28th, 1924.

Waister

In the days of Nelson the largest division in the ship's company was the 'waisters,' stationed in the waist of the ship for manning the various ropes on deck. These men did all the dirty work and were much looked down upon; a man who was good for nothing else was a waister, and the term is nowadays used to describe a man who is worthless.

Wardroom

In 1635 some ships had two gunrooms, each with two guns, one on the lower deck and one on the main deck. Later on, the upper gunroom, from its having the two guns removed, became a sort of storeroom or lumber-room, and it is more than probable that the officers' spare clothes were also stowed there, whence the name 'wardrop' or 'wardrobe' which was appropriated to it, and became corrupted into 'wardroom.'

The subordinate officers' berth was called the 'midshipmen's berth.'

There is no mention of the 'wardroom' as a mess-place for officers till 1758, when the chaplains, who only ranked as warrant officers, petitioned to be allowed to join the wardroom. ('Sea Chaplains' petition to the Lieutenants in the Wardroom.')

The quarter gallery, which opened into it, was used as the repairing shop of the ship's cobbler.

1801
The Midshipman's or British Mariner's Vocabulary, by J. J. Moore, 1801, gives the wardroom as 'A room over the gunroom in ships of war, where the Lieutenants and other principal officers sleep and mess.'

1850
Only in line of battleships and frigates was the mess-place of the senior officers called the 'wardroom.' In smaller ships they messed in the 'gunroom,' and the junior officers in the 'midshipmen's berth.'

Warming the bell

Another expression for 'flogging the clock,' to make it go faster.

Wash-out

This is a term of recent date, and came into use when the signal branch used slates to write down signals, which were later 'washed out.'

Wedding, hoisting a garland

The custom of hoisting a garland when a member of the ship's company is being married can be traced back for two hundred years.

Weevil

A grub found in ship's biscuit. The biscuit, when stored on board, bred a long thin red worm to which the name of 'weevil' was given, from a Royal Naval Victualling Yard of that name. The experienced seaman, when eating his biscuit, always tapped it on the table to allow the big weevils to escape. When the biscuit was very bad it was eaten at night when the eye could not see and the tender heart was spared!

Naval cadets, on being rated midshipmen, had a biscuit broken over their heads in honour of the occasion.

Winger, a

Slang term for a chum.

Wives on board

A certain number of seamen's wives were carried on board at sea all through the year 1700, but this was not so in all ships, and Lord St. Vincent, Nelson and Collingwood were against the practice.

Even at a later date Captains took their wives and families to sea with them.

Yard arm

Recalls that the yard (measure) was measured by the arm of King Henry I of England.

Yard arm, to look out for one's own

To look out for oneself in affairs, possibly with a view to deriving greater benefit than other persons concerned. 'I'm in the boat, shove off,' has much the same meaning, but is used chaffingly to denote indifference to the comfort or point of view of others concerned.

Printed in Great Britain
by Amazon